THE DISENCHANTED

RANDOM HOUSE · NEW YORK

The Disenchanted

A play by BUDD SCHULBERG *and* HARVEY BREIT

(Based on the novel by Budd Schulberg)

DEDICATION

For Pat and Vicki

THE DISENCHANTED *was first presented by William Darrid and Eleanore Saidenberg at the Coronet Theatre, New York City, on December 3, 1958, with the following cast:*

(In order of appearance)

SHEP STEARNS	George Grizzard
VICTOR MILGRIM	Whitfield Connor
MANLEY HALLIDAY	Jason Robards, Jr.
JERE HALLIDAY	Rosemary Harris
SOLDIERS	Richard Kneeland, Michael Del Medico, Moultrie Patten, Larry Ward, Ned Wertimer
GIRLS	Merle Albertson, Nina Clair, Nancy Kovack, Sybil White
BURT SEIXAS	Jason Robards, Sr.
FREDDY	Bernard Kates
GEORGETTE	Salome Jens
WISTER LA SALLE	Jon Cypher
BORIS SHLEPNIKOV	Michael Del Medico
PARTY GUESTS	Merle Albertson, Nina Clair, Richard Kneeland, Nancy Kovack, Moultrie Patten, Larry Ward, Ned Wertimer, Sybil White
DEAN LLEWELLYN	John Leslie
MRS. LLEWELLYN	Eleanor Phelps
PROFESSOR CONNELLY	Salem Ludwig
MRS. CONNELLY	Dorothea Biddle
MR. RIDGEFIELD	Ned Wertimer

Directed by David Pressman

Settings by Ben Edwards

Lighting by Jean Rosenthal

Costumes by Ann Roth

SYNOPSIS OF SCENES

ACT ONE

A winter's evening, 1939.
A beach shack near Malibu Beach.

Old Business: Armistice night, 1918.
A soldiers' canteen, Paris.
  and

Old Business: A Paris garret, 1920.

ACT TWO

Mid-afternoon, a few days later.
Waldorf-Astoria, New York City.

Old Business: December, 1929.
A mansion in Beverly Hills.

ACT THREE

Late afternoon, the following day.
Attic room in Webster College Inn.

Old Business: January, 1930.
A beach cottage, La Jolla, California.

ACT ONE

The curtain rises and the lights come up, revealing MANLEY HALLIDAY's *beach shack. The furnishings are meager. The room is dominated by a work table on which sits a beat-up typewriter. Alongside it is a pile of manuscript. The stage is empty. A knock on the door is heard and* SHEP STEARNS *enters. He is young, perhaps a few years out of college, dressed comfortably and casually.*

STEARNS Mr. Halliday! Mr. Halliday! Mr. Halliday! (SHEP STEARNS *walks into the shack. He looks around with curiosity and a touch of awe. He crosses to the table, taking in its clutter, touches the typewriter respectfully, sits down in* HALLIDAY's *chair and gently types with one finger, as though interested in hearing the sound of the typewriter.* STEARNS *jumps up as* VICTOR MILGRIM *enters. He is expensively dressed and carries with him an air of assurance and success.* STEARNS *addresses him, embarrassed*) Oh, Mr. Milgrim. I was just trying to feel what his typewriter feels like.

MILGRIM He's not here?

STEARNS I knocked and nobody answered so I just walked in.

MILGRIM (*Impatiently*) Are writers unable to be punctual even when they insist on having appointments in their own—

3

quarters? Stearns, the last time I saw Manley Halliday, he was living in a thirty-room mansion overlooking Beverly Hills.

STEARNS Maybe he read my script and walked out into the ocean, like Freddy March at the end of *A Star Is Born*.

MILGRIM (*With mild sarcasm*) I wish my writers would save their humor—such as it is—for their scripts.

STEARNS (*Pointing to a framed snapshot on the desk*) Did you see this? A picture of him with Ernest Hemingway in a fishing boat. "You write good—" signed Ernest . . . How can a Pulitzer Prize winner like Manley Halliday put his name on the available list like any hack?

MILGRIM Stearns, the names that turn up on the available list surprise me constantly.

STEARNS If anyone had predicted that Manley Halliday was going to wind up working on *Love on Ice* with me, I would've said the odds against it were a millon to one. I know what you saw in the idea and I tried my best to give it to you, but what can a novelist like Manley Halliday see in it?

MILGRIM At the moment, Stearns, he doesn't see anything in it. He left word at my office that he and your script are incompatible. That's why I'm here. There are two things a good executive producer must have: the ability to decide on the objective—and then use the personnel best equipped to attain it. My objective with *Love on Ice* is a freshly written college musical that will please the public without offending the college authorities. My choice of personnel—an energetic, disciplined junior writer, teamed with a man who was once the darling of the Ivy League. According to the critics, the only writer ever able to capture the true spirit of American college life. Ten years ago I offered Manley Halliday a small fortune to write for me, and he turned me down with a quip. Ten years—especially his ten years—is a long time. I'm here to change his mind. I've always believed that—(MANLEY HALLI-DAY *enters, carrying a screen play. He is in his early forties and his face reveals the conflict between a perennial youthfulness and the ravages of experience. His clothes, once the height of stylishness, are now a little worn and old-fashioned-looking*) Good to see you, Manley.

(*He crosses to* HALLIDAY *and shake hands*)

HALLIDAY   Hello, Victor; I'm sorry I kept you waiting.

MILGRIM   Not at all. We just arrived. Here's the young man whose magnum opus you've been reading—Shep Stearns.

STEARNS   I still can't believe it. You're really Manley Halliday?

HALLIDAY   You make me sound like one of those three-name writers— Really Manley Halliday. Won't you sit down?

MILGRIM   Thank you. Manley, I won't take no for an answer.

HALLIDAY   Victor, I walked to the end of the beach. I relayed my dilemma to my friends, the sandpipers and the sea gulls, and the answer is still a reluctant no.

MILGRIM (*Ignoring the rejection*) I don't expect to win an Oscar with this one—as I did last year. But I know with your help we can make a pleasing valentine out of it. I think you'll find it an interesting challenge.

HALLIDAY Victor, I don't mind challenges. It may seem erratic; I ask you for a job . . . then I turn you down, but, surely, there must be something you need that I'd be better suited for.

MILGRIM My approach to pictures is this: do a bread-and-butter film like *Love on Ice*—commercially sound, but of course, with what I like to think of as the Milgrim quality. And then, something off-beat, serious, tragic, Dostoievsky, Faulkner —maybe Halliday. But my next picture is *Love on Ice*. (*He pauses to allow his softening-up operation to work; then rapidly presses on*) And I'm prepared to guarantee you ten weeks' work at fifteen hundred dollars a week.

HALLIDAY (*Pensively*) I'd forgotten there were weeks like that.

MILGRIM This could be the start of a very happy relationship. If we score with *Love on Ice*, as I know we can with the Halliday touch, then we'll talk about a forty-week contract at fifteen hundred a week with an escalator clause.

HALLIDAY (*With sardonic humor*) Victor, I don't want to get on your escalator. I'm afraid I might not be able to get off.

MILGRIM If it's money you're after . . .

HALLIDAY I'm not after money, period; I'm after money, comma.

MILGRIM Well, then, take the ten weeks. All I'm asking is a polishing job.

HALLIDAY (*Pacing*) Victor, this script needs more than a polishing job. This script needs a new script.

MILGRIM Then for God's sake, Manley, throw out the whole story line and write it your own way. Even though we hold on to the external values—Webster College, the winter Mardi Gras, the young generation, the ice show, the ski meet—you'd be free to supply the internal values—real people, believable dialogue, wit instead of gags—

HALLIDAY Victor, I feel a little like Faust, torn betwixt angel and devil—and you're both of them.

MILGRIM Isn't any good producer? . . . Manley, with my film sense and your literary genius, we have a chance to create a new form that might revolutionize film musicals.

HALLIDAY (*After a deliberate silence*) *Love on Ice*— May Mr. Pulitzer have mercy on my soul.

MILGRIM Manley, I'm delighted. I'm delighted— I know you'll

7

be pleasantly surprised when you come to the preview. Now let's get down to work. We keep Stearns on—most writers here find it useful to have someone they can bounce ideas against.

HALLIDAY   Sounds like a game of handball. With Stearns here a resilient wall.

STEARNS   I'll be the wall, even the ball itself—anything you need.

HALLIDAY   The grim truth is, I haven't collaborated with anyone since I worked on the Hasty Pudding show of—well—ninety-nine years ago. But I'll try.

MILGRIM (*All business now*)   We happen to have a time pressure on this one. The Mardi Gras comes up this weekend. My second-unit crew will be there covering all the events, but in order for them to shoot intelligently, we would need a step sheet by Friday night.

HALLIDAY   Step sheet?

STEARNS (*Matter-of-factly*)   A step sheet is just an outline of the action step-by-step. It usually isn't more than ten or twelve pages.

HALLIDAY   Deadlines don't bother me. I once wrote a pretty fair novel in a hundred and seven days.

MILGRIM That's incredible . . .

STEARNS *Shadow Ball!* I've been wanting to read that again. Why don't they reprint it? I love that book.

HALLIDAY (*Bitterly*) The critics didn't love it. "Typical of the irresponsibility of the twenties." Quote "In a new decade, Mr. Halliday seems to be entering a strange house to which he was not invited."

STEARNS I know, but some of us thought it was just about the most subtle job of—

MILGRIM (*Interrupting*) This week I don't want you to think about dialogue, or any refinements of the story. You can do all that when you get back.

HALLIDAY Get back? From where?

MILGRIM From Webster. You and Stearns are flying to New York tomorrow.

HALLIDAY (*Startled*) New York?

MILGRIM Yes, I'll catch up with you at the Waldorf on Friday and we'll go up to Webster together.

HALLIDAY (*Troubled*) Victor, I see no earthly reason for working on the script anywhere but here.

MILGRIM   A weekend at Webster will give you a fresh insight into this new generation of college kids.

HALLIDAY   They're still the same little savages I used to know. Besides, Stearns here ought to know how his generation looks and talks and thinks.

MILGRIM   Manley, it's not as if I were asking you to go to Tibet or Shangrila.

STEARNS   You fasten your safety belt, you take a couple of slugs of whiskey, and you're there. Today it's around the corner.

HALLIDAY   (*Softly*)   Ten leagues beyond . . . the wide world's end . . . (*Agitatedly*)   For me it's far. It's very far.

MILGRIM   This is beyond argument. I already took the liberty of arranging a meeting with the dean and a few of his colleagues on Saturday at five. I want you with me. Out here we think in terms of Academy Awards, but at Webster they seem to put even more weight on Pulitzer Prizes.

HALLIDAY   Victor, you're hiring me as a writer, not as a roving ambassador of good will.

MILGRIM   Oh, nonsense—it's just that I want my people where I need them. Now, don't be stubborn, Manley.

HALLIDAY   I'm not stubborn. I'm just stationary. Planes and Pullman cars give me bad dreams.

MILGRIM (*Suspiciously, but suavely*)   There's nothing wrong with you? A screen writer needs a strong back as well as a good mind. You have been taking care of yourself?

HALLIDAY (*Indignation, mounting to anger*)   Victor, I'm too old for euphemisms. Am I positively off the booze? That's what you mean, isn't it? For two hundred seventy-nine days I have been drinking nothing stronger than Sunkist orange juice. (*He pulls out a whiskey bottle from a closet*) Take a good look at this bottle—a decent, well-behaved bottle—it's lived with me for nine months and still a virgin . . . I've learned to eat and sleep and live and work on this workbench. I function here. I don't have to go out into the world. I've had the world. I can bring it here.

MILGRIM   I'm not asking you to disrupt your life. All I'm asking is that you put in three days in New York.

HALLIDAY (*Obsessively*)   Why New York? Why three days in New York?

MILGRIM   Manley, how long has it been since you watched those kids meet under the Biltmore clock or studied the girls pouring into Grand Central to catch the *Mardi Gras Special*? I want you to move with them to Webster, seeing it with them, writing it with their young hearts and their young eyes.

HALLIDAY (*Wryly*)   Help me, Cassius, or I sink.

MILGRIM (*Laughing unhappily*)   Exactly one week from today you'll be back here again.

STEARNS Seven short days, Mr. Halliday. We'll make them fly.

HALLIDAY New York and I have had an old-fashioned divorce. We don't even talk to each other any more. I'm finished with Manhattan—and Staten Island, too.

MILGRIM There must be something about this you're not telling me.

HALLIDAY Isn't there always? Victor, I'm not telling you. I'm asking you to let me do this piece of work here, where we are now, right here.

MILGRIM (*Sits and begins to write out a check*) Manley, I'm due back at the studio to see today's rushes. I want to leave your first week's check. I'm making it—two thousand dollars. My top salary for my top writers.
  (*He hands the check to* HALLIDAY)

HALLIDAY I'm sorry I can't oblige you, Victor. I'm sorry I can't oblige myself.

MILGRIM (*Urbanely*) Hold on to it. If, in the morning, you decide not to keep it, simply return it to my office. Well, it's wonderful seeing you again. Good night, Manley.

HALLIDAY Good night, Victor.

MILGRIM (*Walks to the door*) I'm counting on your coming to

Webster with me. (*Studiedly casual*) By the way, you have a tuxedo. The dinner for us on Saturday night is black tie.
(MILGRIM *exits*)

HALLIDAY (*After a brief silence*)   What a lovely world this must have been before Victor Milgrim invented money. (*He crumples the check and throws it into the wastebasket.* STEARNS *picks up his manuscript and quietly starts for the door. At the door he pauses and turns in a mute appeal, but* HALLIDAY'S *back is to him. He reaches for the knob.* HALLIDAY *speaks, without looking up*) So you read *Shadow Ball?*

STEARNS (*Spinning around*)   Mr. Halliday, please come to New York with me! *Shadow Ball. Friends and Foes. The Lamps along the Park. Friends and Foes* was my bible. Mr. Halliday, it's my first writing job. I waited three years for this chance. I took a hundred odd jobs and wrote movie scripts at night in order to break through, and now I've finally done it.

HALLIDAY (*Takes scenario, holds it*)   That's your ambition—to be a movie writer?

STEARNS   After *Love on Ice* you probably don't think I'm any kind of a writer at all.

HALLIDAY   This script is dreadful, Stearns, but every few pages I hear your voice—good, isolated bits that stick out of your script like pylons.

STEARNS   Thank you, Mr. Halliday.

13

HALLIDAY   But the question is, Stearns, where was *Love on Ice* born? Not inside you—not inside Victor Milgrim. It is a celluloid baby, born of artificial insemination on a box-office counter.

STEARNS   But you can't condemn the whole medium because of this one. Serious movies combine all the arts—and they carry a hell of a message all over the world. It's practically the first international language. Look at Chaplin, *The Informer, Ten Days That Shook the World*— I have no illusions about this one, but if what you feel about me is true, I can say a little more the next time out, and then a little more after that and then—one of these days I can do a picture I really believe in— about the dust bowl, Mexican wetbacks . . .

HALLIDAY   Ever higher and higher! Don't you see you're kidding yourself? If you write three bad scripts, the fourth will be worse, not better. The mask becomes the face, whether in politics or art . . . Remember that.

STEARNS   Okay, Mr. Halliday . . . Right now I'm only worried about this one. If you take it on it'll be a different story. We can raise it above a pot boiler . . .

HALLIDAY   If only I didn't have to take on New York.

STEARNS   Look, we'll lock ourselves in, we won't even know we're in New York.

HALLIDAY   New York will know I'm in New York.

STEARNS (*Vigorously*) I'll pull up the drawbridge. I'll stand guard at the door. (*Shyly*) I'll type like a tiger.

HALLIDAY (*Appreciatively*) Frankly, I'm surprised to find anyone of your generation who even remembers *Friends and Foes*.

STEARNS Are you kidding? Boy, when Milgrim told me there was a chance I'd work with you it was like telling me I might work with Thomas Hardy or Joseph Conrad. In fact, when I first heard about it, I didn't think you were still . . .
(*He halts awkwardly*)

HALLIDAY Still alive? Reports of my death have been exaggerated—or should I say only slightly exaggerated.

STEARNS Boy, what made me think that? Maybe because the pace of those times was so fast and you caught it so well, that when the jazz age died—

HALLIDAY Why do you remember only the party scenes? It wasn't all gin and confetti. I wrote other things, too.

STEARNS I used to quote that whole chapter on the argument between General Pershing and the Unknown Soldier. Funny, when I was working my way through Webster, we were all for proletarian literature. We used to tear you apart as middle-class, decadent, defeatist. But late at night, alone in my room, I found myself thinking through your ideas, living out your experiences, knowing your characters better than I knew my roommates. And your heroines—I fell in love with them all. What a parade of marvelous girls! That Leonore Woodbury. The way you first brought her in, wearing that polar-bear coat and nothing but that polar-bear coat. She was so real my dates used to get jealous, I talked so much about her. I suppose you've been asked this a thousand times, but was Leonore a real person? Did you really know a golden-eyed jazz-baby like that?

HALLIDAY (*Troubled*) No . . . she wasn't a real person.

(JERE *laughs, offstage.* HALLIDAY *appears haunted and dazed. Since* JERE *exists only in his mind, her laughter is not heard by* STEARNS)

STEARNS I thought I read somewhere she was based on your wife.

HALLIDAY (*Hypnotically*) She was fiction. She bears no relation to any person living or dead. JERE's *laugh is heard offstage again*) She was a fiction. I created her from the champagne threads and vapors of the times.

(*The past begins to encroach on the present: as the foreground lights dim and the background lights come up, a Paris army canteen establishes itself right in the shack, and behind it a Parisian street is visible. Simultaneous with this gradual change, couples in uniform dance into the beach shack to the music of "Smiles" played by a piano and a trumpet. Couples in uniform are laughing and singing and shouting "Fini la guerre" and "Vive*

l'armistice." STEARNS *is lost in the foreground shadows.*
JERE *dances in with an American soldier. She is a beautiful*
girl, with red-gold hair, dressed in a lovely ball gown of
the period. Although HALLIDAY *is still in his beach-shack*
clothes, he now wears them as though they were the
uniform of a young captain. Now he is the attractive
MANLEY HALLIDAY *of 1918*)

JERE (*Just coming on*)   I feel champagne-yellow tonight!

HALLIDAY   I said over and over she's fictitious. She never ex-
isted. She wasn't true.

FIRST SOLDIER   Peace. Peace!

SECOND SOLDIER   *La guerre est fini!*
(JERE *dances in flirtatiously, and several adoring soldiers*
pick her up and carry her around the room with mock
pomp and circumstance)

JERE (*Regally*)   I declare a holiday throughout the realm! Let
the slaves drink wine!
(*She is put down amid cheers.* HALLIDAY *approaches her*)

HALLIDAY   You are the most beautiful woman I have ever seen.

JERE (*With a broad French accent*)   That is not important.
(*They stand, fascinated by each other, as the other couples*
dance and continue to celebrate behind them)

HALLIDAY   Perhaps mademoiselle will be good enough to say what is important.

JERE   Dancing. Pleasure. To be gay—these are the only truths.

HALLIDAY   But are you not too attractive to bother about definitions of truth?

JERE   Ho-hum.

HALLIDAY   I bore you?

JERE   Being told I'm beautiful? Why shouldn't it bore me? Generals and privates tell me. Even handsome captains. (HALLIDAY *salutes smartly*) I have eyes. I can see that I am beautiful. I look into the glass after the bath and I say to myself, "How much more beautiful you are than those stupid pink nudes of Renoir."

HALLIDAY   Perhaps some day soon I shall be fortunate enough to be permitted to agree with you.

JERE   Ish kabibble.

HALLIDAY   Hah. So you've picked up some of our slang.

JERE   Yes, these slang is, how you say, very funnee of uz—what you call bed-pillow French.

Jason Robards, Jr., and Rosemary Harris,
as MANLEY and JERE HALLIDAY

HALLIDAY You're not French. Come clean now. Who are you? What do you do? Why aren't you in uniform?

JERE I will tell you a secret but do not be frightened. I am a sorceress.

HALLIDAY Apprentice or professional?

JERE It's Armistice Night—let them court-martial me! If I have to face a firing squad I'll die as a woman—not as a corporal—

HALLIDAY Rebellious and lovely corporal—I salute you! Don't leave me! Don't vanish. (*The music stops. She moves toward the crowd*) *Sittensie!* I have got to talk to you.
(*They sit facing each other across the table*)

JERE I like intense men. Who are you?

HALLIDAY Some days I'm Christopher Wren building my own cathedral. Some nights I'm Toulouse-Lautrec on the prowl with paints and brushes. I might even try to be a writer.

JERE That's it. You are a writer.

HALLIDAY How do you know?

JERE It's the one you find hardest to say.

HALLIDAY (*Thoughtfully quiet*) ... One day I met a German soldier in Belleau Wood leaning against a shattered tree, writing a sonnet. And we talked about Schiller.

JERE In the very eye of the holocaust two enemies meet and talk quietly together about Schiller. And your commander would have hated you both.

HALLIDAY If I could be a novelist, that's what I'd write about.

JERE *Friends and Foes*. That's your novel!

HALLIDAY *Friends and Foes,* by Manley Halliday!... I like it.

JERE (*Standing up*) Then, Manley Halliday, write it! I'll make you write it. If you don't, I'll haunt you.
    (*She waves her hands over his head as if casting a spell*)

HALLIDAY (*Standing up and facing her*) Who are you?

JERE I am me and me is I—
    Lawless, flawless Lorelei—
    If I should die before I try—
    Will you put a penny on my eye?

HALLIDAY You'll never die. You're my eternal jazz-baby Lorelei.

JERE Oh, I love writers ... I've loved hundreds of them. (HALLIDAY *retreats indignantly*) Such a grim look, m'sieur. You

are not by any chance an agent of the Sûreté?
(*She backs away*)

HALLIDAY (*Following her*) Madam—I have been shadowing
you for years. Your name is Hilda Von Fruhling-Spitzel
Horsthausenschaft, Operator Thirty-two X!

JERE *Ach, Ausgefundet!* (*"Till We Meet Again" is played*)
That's the last song; I have to leave you and say good night
to everybody.

HALLIDAY Don't be so gregarious.

JERE It's my job. I'll tell you a secret—I love my job. I wish
that wars would go on and on and on, only without any shooting, so that these patriotic orgies would go on and on too. It
makes me feel so conscientiously promiscuous.

HALLIDAY Just be promiscuous with me.

SOLDIER Come on, Jere, we're going on to the Ritz Bar.

HALLIDAY (*Ushering crowd out good-naturedly*) We'll catch
up with you in an hour. Just tell them at the Ritz that the
Armistice isn't official until General Pershing and Gracie
Fields arrive. (*They all laugh, and the soldiers and girls exit,
some singing "There's a long, long trail."* HALLIDAY *and* JERE
stare at each other for a moment in silence) Never imagined
that there were eyes like yours. Blind as turquoise and seeing

as a cat. (*Kneels left of her*) Or as though your eyes were made to see something other than objects. You do see, don't you, Jere . . . What do you see?

JERE (*Mystically*) I see spinning. I see the world spinning. I see inside you spinning.

HALLIDAY Should I take you seriously?

JERE Never completely . . . but always a little.

HALLIDAY (*Seriously*) I'll always remember that.

JERE "*O terrible frisson des amours novices sur le sol sanglant!*" Oh, the agony of new love on bleeding earth. Rimbaud and bright lights never seem right together. He wrote by the light of hellfire! (HALLIDAY *turns off the overhead lamp*) One of these days I'm going to astonish the world with my translations. But now when I try to put Rimbaud into English it goes so dingy and—blah!

HALLIDAY Then why try?

JERE I love to dive deep. I need to climb high.

HALLIDAY I never wanted anyone or anything so much.
(*He takes her in his arms*)

JERE It's three in the morning, my lipstick's all smeared, my hair's a mess, I feel older than Elsie Janis' mother—and you still want to seduce me?

HALLIDAY Your mouth is my hunger. I can hear the wine singing, and you're the youngest old-enough girl in the world. And I'm all the determined young men.

JERE And I'm all the undetermined young women. That's dangerous.

HALLIDAY (*Kisses her*) Jere ... Jere ...
  (*In his passion he begins to unbutton her dress*)

JERE Mannie, I hate that feeling ... fingers under my clothes.

HALLIDAY Jere ... please. Please!

JERE When it happens, we'll both know and we'll come to each other and our clothes will fall away.

HALLIDAY Jere, you must! You must!

JERE There isn't anything in this world that I must! Except die. And I'll never forgive God for that!

HALLIDAY You'll never die. You're ageless and timeless. Promise me you'll look exactly as you do this moment a hundred years from now.

JERE (*Backing away slowly and sensuously*)   Mannie, I promise . . . I promise.
(*The Paris scene fades as* JERE *backs off and disappears. The lights change and we are once again in the present with* STEARNS *and* HALLIDAY)

HALLIDAY (*Upset, striking the table sharply*)   She wasn't true, I tell you. She wasn't true!

STEARNS (*Uneasily*)   The critics sure convinced a lot of us . . .

HALLIDAY   I don't care what the critics say. Oh, why in God's name don't the critics write about the sins in our books instead of titillating the public with our personal lives. I'm through with personal lives. Until today, no more than two people crossed the threshold in the last nine months.

STEARNS   How did you ever wind up in a—hideout like this?

HALLIDAY   One day I was twenty-eight—and the next day I was forty. And when you're forty, you think about all the books you should have written. How little time there is left to do them in. On my fortieth birthday, I hadn't worked on a book for eight years. I found myself walking along the beach, until I came here. It looked like me. Ramshackle—on shaky stilts, a few leaks in the roof. This is where I make my stand, I told myself. I went into training: tough daily workouts on that Corona; eat, work, walk, sleep—eat, work, work—
(*He falters and, with* STEARNS' *help, lowers himself into a chair*)

STEARNS   What is it? You'd better sit down.

HALLIDAY   Sorry. Look—get out of here. I'll be all right.

STEARNS   You want me to call a doctor?

HALLIDAY   (*Gaining control*) I can handle it. Sugar in the blood. Should have used the old needle and taken my insulin. Portrait of the artist as a middle-aged ascetic. When I fall behind this way I get shaky . . . wish I could turn this model in for a new chassis.

STEARNS   Is this why you can't come to New York, Mr. Halliday?

HALLIDAY   New York is a terrible chance and it's too late for chances. The stakes are too high.

STEARNS   Sure they're high, but together we're a cinch to satisfy Milgrim.

HALLIDAY   Do you think I'd subject myself to the ignominy of Victor Milgrim's available list if I didn't have an end beyond the end of merely satisfying Milgrim? No, Stearns, no. These are the stakes I'm talking about!
(*He strikes his piled-up manuscript*)

STEARNS   (*Drawn to the manuscript, reading*) *Folly and Farewell.* You're writing again . . . you've got a book!

HALLIDAY It's what I've been dragging along with me all my life . . . Please! Don't read that! Nobody can read that until it's finished.

(STEARNS *steps away from the table*)

STEARNS I'm sorry, Mr. Halliday . . . I think it's wonderful news.

HALLIDAY It would be better news if I ever got it done.

STEARNS When did you start writing again? Is it going well?

HALLIDAY (*Ironically*) Oh, I've been writing—letters to creditors, explaining why checks are not enclosed, and to an angry army of bill collectors the same message. Oh, I've been writing.

STEARNS You mean, with a Halliday novel in that Corona you can't get your publishers to get you off the hook? After all your fantastic success?

HALLIDAY Fantastic success! But commit the unforgivable sin of failure and the temple doors are slammed in your face— the gods of Manhattan are more ruthless than Jehovah. Stearns, on my last visit to New York I stayed in a third-class hotel and ate Fig Newtons. I couldn't call my best friend in the world—my editor, Burt Seixas—because I owed him two thousand I knew he could use. I was afraid to go down to the lobby for fear that some enterprising sob sister would trap me for one of those riches-to-rags human-interest yarns. Nothing fails like success. God, I hate that city.

STEARNS   But this time it has to be different! The Waldorf, a Milgrim picture, a fat expense account—that's the way to go to New York. What a place it is . . . the life of that city.

HALLIDAY   The dead of that city . . . and the crazy thing is I know I'm on to the one big book of my life. I'll show them: the doubters, the scoffers and, goddamn them, the forgetters! The trick is to endure.

STEARNS   (*Jumping up excitedly*)   Look, if this movie job is the only way back to the book, I'd be damned if I'd let anything scare me off it. Not New York, not Milgrim, not Webster, not my *Love on Ice,* not nothing. I'd just let it roll off my back. I'd do anything I had to as good as I can, as fast as I can, and get back to the book.

HALLIDAY   Not so fast, Stearns. The choice is slower and harder than that. Six months ago I made your decision: a quick job so I could clear the decks for my last big war. But should a man do less than he is able to do? I worry about that. I keep thinking that every time a man betrays his total gift, his unique ability, the universe fails.

STEARNS   I don't think the universe ever fails. At its worst, maybe it falters—that's it, it falters. You'll come back to your book and you won't have to cheat on it. You can be faithful to it, because you'll come back with a clean bank account, a

27

free mind and a clear conscience. (*He picks the crumpled check out of the wastebasket*) Just multiply two thousand dollars times ten weeks and you've got it. Don't you see you've got it?

HALLIDAY   Ten weeks times two thousand dollars makes twenty thousand dollars—minus agent's fee leaves eighteen thousand, and taxes takes it to sixteen thousand eight hundred ... (*He begins to work it out on paper*) ... Jere's hospital and alimony leaves ... thirteen thousand four ... and Douglas' tuition and allowance makes it twelve thousand ... then the one-must-pay-back personal debt, which leaves seventy-three hundred dollars—seven thousand three hundred dollars clear. (*He takes the manuscript from the table and talks to it*) My friend, I may have to leave you for a while, but don't get discouraged, don't go away, you bastard. I'll be back.

STEARNS (*With sudden realization*)   Then you're going to go?

HALLIDAY (*Quietly*)   It'll be like making a pilgrimage to my own grave.

STEARNS (*Wildly*)   Oh ... this calls for a drink! Oh, I forgot ...

HALLIDAY (*Amiably*)   That's all right. You can do the drinking for both of us.

STEARNS   It's a dream, going back to the old Alma Mater with Manley Halliday. Boy, will the old school eat that up!

HALLIDAY Say when.

STEARNS Okay. When! To our first Oscar! Who's Hecht and MacArthur? To Halliday and Stearns!

HALLIDAY (*Trying to capture* STEARNS' *mood*) The Rover Boys at the Waldorf.

STEARNS The Rover Boys at Webster!

HALLIDAY (*Asking for reassurance*) It's going to be all right?

STEARNS Oh, it's going to be a lot better than all right! According to the Milgrim Law of Cinematics, with your brain and my back we ought to make one hell of a screen writer.
     (*His enthusiasm is infectious*)

HALLIDAY Let's give Milgrim not only the Milgrim quality, but something better than that.

STEARNS Sold! We'll knock them dead on Saturday at five o'clock in the afternoon.

HALLIDAY Ah, that fatal five in the afternoon. The Dove and the Leopard wrestled at five in the afternoon.

STEARNS It was five o'clock by all the clocks. It was five in the shade of the afternoon.

HALLIDAY Our first collaboration. (*Excitedly, after they both laugh happily*) Stearns . . . Shep, Shep—Shep! It's beginning to work. I'm going to sit down and wind up that obstinate Chapter Six tonight. When I come back I'll be all set for Part Two of *Folly and Farewell*. Oh, God, I feel like a writer again.

STEARNS Great! Work well, my first and best collaborator. (*He strides to the door*) I'll pick you up at the crack of dawn in Victor Milgrim's Cadillac. You'll recognize it because it's painted green . . . like money!
  (STEARNS *exits*)

HALLIDAY (*Sitting down to work*) The fundamental character of everyone . . . the bottom-dog nature in them . . . the strength and weakness in them . . . the color of their moods . . . the living and the loving!
  (JERE *enters as the lights change, bringing with her a sense of the past. They are in a Paris studio in the early twenties.* JERE *carries a new hat*)

JERE Darling, I feel all aquamarine today.

HALLIDAY (*Lovingly*) Go away. Leave me alone.
  (*He sprawls on his stomach and tries to write*)

JERE Darling, I have a delicious surprise for you.

HALLIDAY I haven't time to think about you today.

JERE (*Modeling the hat*) Look—isn't it madly elegant? I bought it for you. I want my husband to ravish me in my Reboux hat. The four hundred francs we saved for bread and sausage . . . it's on my head. On this head sits our entire menu for a week. Doesn't that prove we're not earthbound?

HALLIDAY Our last four hundred francs. Jere, you moon-struck desperado. What am I going to do with you?

JERE Thank me, darling. My extravagance will bring us luck. The time to celebrate a triumph is before it happens, because —that will make it happen. Tomorrow the world will go out of its mind over *Friends and Foes*.

HALLIDAY I love you.

JERE Champagne at Maxim's. We'll be so rich we won't need money.

HALLIDAY You soothsaying dunce . . . what am I going to do with you?

JERE Waltz me at midnight to the *Rosenkavalier*—

HALLIDAY Go away!

JERE There was a time . . . last week . . . when my being in the next room was too far.

HALLIDAY   I love you through the wall, but tonight I need an hour. Go and fix Rimbaud. Knock him dead.

JERE   That horrible, wonderful Rimbaud. I'm giving him up. I've decided that if people want to read Rimbaud, let them learn French . . . I'll finish my Rimbaud if you take me to Rapallo, where I'll overwhelm Ezra Pound with my translations. And then we'll both be rich and famous.

HALLIDAY   We'll never be rich and famous if you don't let me work.

JERE   But I feel fabulous and wicked.

HALLIDAY   Go away—not far away, just far enough. For an hour. One big hour. One ten-week hour.
   (*The lights begin to change again, suggesting that the past is slowly giving way to the present*)

JERE (*Ecstatic*)   We'll go to every warm corner of the world.

HALLIDAY (*Determined*)   Ten weeks in hell—I'll make them fly.

JERE   In the mornings we'll walk naked into the sea.

HALLIDAY   Then back to the living and the loving . . .

JERE   In the afternoons . . .

HALLIDAY   Ten furious months ...

JERE   We'll flirt with the dolphins.

HALLIDAY   I'll make them count.

JERE   In the evenings we'll whisper at sidewalk tables.

HALLIDAY   A second chance!

JERE   And in the nights ...

HALLIDAY   I can do it!

JERE   In the nights ...

HALLIDAY   I can do it!

JERE   Oh, Manley—in the nights!

HALLIDAY (*A little less certain*)   I can do it!

Curtain

ACT TWO

ACT TWO

Friday afternoon, four days later, a suite in the Waldorf. STEARNS *is typing in the sitting room. The floor is littered with discarded balled-up paper. He is interrupted by a knock on the door.*

STEARNS (*Rushing to the door*) Manley! Where—
  (*He opens the door.* BURT SEIXAS *enters. He is a middle-aged man of medium height, on the unpressed, tweedy side, with something of the library about him*)

SEIXAS I'm Burt Seixas, an old friend of Manley's.

STEARNS Oh, you're Manley's editor. Come on in! I'm Stearns.

SEIXAS I read about you and Manley in the morning paper— not without a certain qualm. Isn't Manley here?

STEARNS He went out to get some air. Let me have your coat. It's been rough. We've been cooped up for three days in this Park Avenue trap. His complexion was about the color of this—it's one thing we've plenty of—blank paper.

SEIXAS Your graveyard of dead ideas. Only two kinds of writing come easy. A natural writer expressing himself and a natural hack with no self to express.

STEARNS (*Exasperated*) The only self being expressed around here is Victor Milgrim. Look at these telegrams. "Please phone me soonest you think you have story line worth discussing. See you Friday. Warmest regards. Victor." Here's the last one. "Worried by your silence. This is Friday." It doesn't even say regards and it's signed Milgrim.

SEIXAS Does he have to send you a wire to tell you what day it is? How is Manley taking New York? He doesn't seem too upset?

STEARNS He's not chasing chambermaids down corridors. But his mind—it keeps chasing ghosts!

SEIXAS Down the corridors of his past.

STEARNS Yeah, yeah, that's it! I never met anyone who—roots around in his memory so much. The past is right on his skin!

SEIXAS I worry about his ghosts in New York.

STEARNS Won't you sit down . . . On his way out just now he had the strangest look on his face—as if there was a ghost waiting out there for him.

SEIXAS (*Tapping his pipe*) Mr. Stearns! There haven't been any phone calls at crazy hours—four or five in the morning?

STEARNS Yeah. We did have a couple. But we decided it was that insomniac Milgrim, so we let it ring.

SEIXAS   He wasn't anxious about a call from anyone else?

STEARNS   Mr. Seixas, our anxiety for this week is Victor Milgrim.

SEIXAS   He didn't say anything about seeing his wife—Jere?

STEARNS   From everything he's told me, she's the last person he'd want to see.

SEIXAS   She was always the last person he wanted to see and she was always the first person he did see.

STEARNS   (*Agitated*)   Do you think that's where he's gone?

SEIXAS   I hope to God not. The last time he came to New York I begged him not to see her, but—of course he did. It was a nightmare. Manley disappeared. I hunted for him in three states. I hate to tell you what condition I found him in.

STEARNS   (*After a momentary pause, quietly*)   Oh, my God! Now and then it hits me how sure I am about what I don't know . . . Between Milgrim's telegrams and Manley's ghosts I'll be an old man at twenty-six. Here, Mr. Seixas, you can publish them—"The Collected Telegrams of Victor Milgrim." (*Shouting crazily*) Manley . . . where the hell are you? . . . I'm sorry, Mr. Manley . . . Mr. Seixas. You see, I think I'm going out of my mind. On Monday I was a normal, healthy, well-adjusted junior writer. You want to play a game of chess?

SEIXAS   Stearns, has Manley been drinking?

STEARNS   No, not a drop. He's solidly on the wagon!

SEIXAS   Thank God! I always worry about that when he's near Jere.

STEARNS (*Indignantly*)   What happens? Every time he climbs up she drags him down?

SEIXAS   It was never as simple as something one did to the other. It was always the two of them doing it to each one of them. They danced in a champagne haze on the rooftop of the world. Jere could have made a first-rate poet if she had any discipline or any confidence. They always had too much money and always needed more. She could do so many things so brilliantly and all the time she was a failure, and though it seemed incredible at the time, he was failing, too. He caught the writer's most dreaded disease—silence—years and years of silence. I could never get him started again.

STEARNS   But he has started again!

SEIXAS   This movie?

STEARNS   No, I'm talking about a novel.

SEIXAS (*Rising with excitement*)   What makes you think he's working on a novel?

STEARNS I saw it. I touched it. He carries it around as if it were a live bird in his pocket.

SEIXAS That's my old Manley! You sure?

STEARNS Yeah, he's calling it *Folly and Farewell.*

SEIXAS After all these years. That manuscript has been accident-prone. One draft was lost on a train. Another version he tossed into the sea. "Flaubert wouldn't have liked it," he said. A third time . . . there was a third time.

STEARNS (*Moving toward his typewriter*) I wish to hell he'd come back. I can feel Milgrim's propeller slicing off the top of my head.

SEIXAS (*Walking to the telephone*) I'd better phone Jere.
(HALLIDAY *enters unobtrusively. He is elegantly dressed in his best clothes of ten years before. He looks fresh and revived*)

HALLIDAY You can call off the bloodhounds!

STEARNS Boy, am I glad to see you!

HALLIDAY (*Slowly and noncommittally approaching* SEIXAS) It was such a fine day I decided to walk to the Plaza. I renewed my acquaintance with the fountain, had a chat with a distinguished old horse, who reminded me of the days when we used to take hansom cabs at four o'clock in the morning. (*He embraces* SEIXAS *with great warmth*) Burt, you old bastard!

SEIXAS (*Embracing* HALLIDAY)   Manley, you old wanderer!

HALLIDAY   Let me look at you. You're wearing that same old jacket and that same old tie and—the same old Dunhill Willa Cather gave you.

SEIXAS   And you still have those same precocious school-boy eyes. (*Turns to* STEARNS) I remember when he came into my office with his first novel ... those eyes reflected such impossible assurance, I made up my mind to dislike the book. But the book insisted on being liked.
   (*They laugh*)

STEARNS   Manley, we got another wire. Any minute now we'll be getting his messages in person.

HALLIDAY   Give me five minutes. Shep, I wasn't just talking to horses on my walk, I even had a few notions about *Love on Ice*.

STEARNS   Okay. I'll grab a shower and we'll crack it this time. Mr. Seixas, nice to meet you.
   (*He exits into bedroom*)

SEIXAS   Manley, Manley, after all these years! After the fire I heard a thousand conflicting stories from a thousand different friends.

HALLIDAY   I never had a thousand friends—I had nine hundred and ninety-nine hangers-on and you.

SEIXAS   Well, the past is past. You've survived fire and ice— And now, you secretive, conspiratorial so-and-so, you're writing again, you're rewriting *Folly and Farewell*. I'll take the first chapters with me and go over them tonight.

HALLIDAY   (*After a brief pause*)   No.

SEIXAS   What do you mean no? Why shouldn't I plunge right in tonight?

HALLIDAY   No, Burt, no! Not until I've written the last word.

SEIXAS   Come on, now—none of your guff.

HALLIDAY   (*Pacing the room*)   Burt, it's as simple as this: I don't want you fighting for my unfinished symphonies ever again, suffering through those announcements of a new Halliday novel for the fall list, the spring list, the never-never list. I want to be able to come to you and say, here it is, all finished, and I defy you to find one lifeless word, one inexact phrase, one idle gesture. Burt, I have a book! It's all there, in these palms. No matter how long I go with my hands in my pockets, the book is still there, in these hands, and I can pick it up as though I've never been away.

SEIXAS   It's awesome how much you sound like the old Manley.

43

HALLIDAY   Like the older Manley.

SEIXAS   For God's sake, be careful. These expeditions can be treacherous. My phone hasn't stopped ringing.

HALLIDAY (*Sadly*)   On my way back from the Plaza I found myself walking up and down Jere's street. I even pressed the little black button next to her name, but when she buzzed back I turned around and ran.

SEIXAS   Now that you've decided to survive, you've got to think of her as dead.

HALLIDAY   What do you think I've been trying to do these last ten years?

SEIXAS   I never said it was easy. But you've got to dedicate yourself to yourself.

HALLIDAY   I'm trying! More than trying—I'm doing it.

SEIXAS (*He takes his hat and coat and goes to the door*)   That's good enough for me. You sure you won't change your mind and let me see what you've got done, just for old time's sake?

HALLIDAY   For new time's sake, let me do it my way.

SEIXAS   All right, Manley . . . Don't answer that telephone! (*He exits*)

44

HALLIDAY (*After a pause*) C'mon, Shep, let's get on the ball! I'm for cracking this thing! (*In a half-whisper*) Besides, I've got used to not being alone . . .

STEARNS (*Briskly entering*) Hey, you're picking up the jive pretty good. Now let's have one of those ideas you got off that old horse in the park.

HALLIDAY Well, somehow they sounded better out of doors.

STEARNS (*Disappointed*) This is indoors . . . Why don't we take another look at some of the starts we've had—bad, lousy and indifferent. (*He crosses to* HALLIDAY *with the wastebasket.* HALLIDAY *takes it and selects a crumpled ball of paper*) One of them just might do it. (*The telephone rings.* STEARNS *takes it up slowly*) Hello . . . oh! Just a minute, I'll see— It's Mrs. Halliday.

HALLIDAY (*Whispering urgently*) I'm not in! I'm not in!

STEARNS Sorry, I don't see him in his room. He must've gone out . . . I don't know when he'll be back. Yeah. (*He hangs up, troubled*) Manley, do you mind if I ask you a question?

HALLIDAY Yes! Now let's get back to work.

STEARNS (*He reads from one of the crumpled papers on the table*) Boy, this one hasn't improved with age . . . (*He looks at another as* HALLIDAY *reads his page with difficulty*) Say,

45

what if we go back to my waitress? This time she's not a gum-chewer. She's sort of a social-register Hepburn type who's had a hassle with her old man. He threw her out and . . .

HALLIDAY Have you ever heard of a waitress who turned out main line?

STEARNS Hell, if you applied that test to every script, you'd have no movies.

HALLIDAY What I want to know is what makes a girl like that do a thing like that. I knew a girl on Long Island who was brought up in the most proper blue-stocking way. Even when she was eighteen her parents had to approve her beaux and she had to be home by eleven. It was the insecurity that comes with money. Who will love me for myself alone? When she busted out, it was a Vesuvius. Last I heard of her . . .

STEARNS (*Jumping up with excitement*) Say! That's an idea. We get a girl who's in the middle of an adolescent rebellion, really wild! I knew a girl like that. A sixteen-year-old kid, daughter of a minister across the river from Webster, and hot as a pistol. Polly Ann Dean! The boys called her Dizzy. One night a quarterback brought her into the dorm and sold chances on her. She stayed nine days and that boy made his tuition.

HALLIDAY (*Laughing*) Dizzy Dean! That's a good one!

STEARNS   The campus cops moved in and took Dizzy home. The quarterback was expelled.

HALLIDAY   Oh, that's too bad.

STEARNS (*Quietly*)   He was only third string.

HALLIDAY (*After a pause, thoughtfully*)   For the movies we might have to clean it up a little. We could get Jeanette Mac-Donald and give her a few songs to sing.

STEARNS (*Laughing*)   MacDonald would be terrific! We could get George Raft for the boy. Poor third-string quarterback working his way through college.
   (*He flips an imaginary coin in the familiar Raft manner*)

HALLIDAY   With Peter Lorre as an exchange student!. . . He's majoring in Krafft-Ebing and Advanced Rape One.

STEARNS (*Approaching* HALLIDAY)   Lorre's date is Mae West. She's a freshman at Smith. Her mother warned her about those Webster wolves.

HALLIDAY (*Standing up*)   So she rooms with Dizzy because she thinks she'll be safe with the minister's daughter. Instead of *Love on Ice,* we'll call it *Dizzy's Raffle-Dazzle.*
   (*They laugh together*)

STEARNS (*Explosively breaking his laughter*)   Aw, come on! I feel like Huck Finn, laughing at my own funeral.

HALLIDAY I'm sorry.

STEARNS (*Going to the typewriter*) So am I! Let's get back to work.
(*There is a momentary silence.* HALLIDAY, *grimacing, picks up another crumpled sheet from the wastebasket*)

HALLIDAY (*Chuckling quietly*) I remember once I had a fierce deadline in St. Moritz and Jere . . .

STEARNS Honestly, Manley, couldn't we give up on all that? This is now. I know it's dull as hell, but this is Victor Milgrim's generation and he's on my back.

HALLIDAY Okay, laddie, okay, okay, okay. Let's box it. I feel a little of Victor Milgrim's breath on my neck too. And it makes me sick.

STEARNS (*Anxiously*) Did you take your insulin?

HALLIDAY Remind me later. I'll take it later.

STEARNS Can you work without it? I keep coming back to the script.

HALLIDAY (*With sudden confidence*) The script! We're going to be all right on that.

STEARNS (*Puzzled and impatient*) How? Tell me how we'll be all right on that?

HALLIDAY (*Mysteriously*) The blue sky-rack! That's what we've got to get now. We've got to get that blue sky-rack.

STEARNS (*Disbelieving*) What's the blue sky-rack?

HALLIDAY (*Inspired*) It's something you pull out of the blue. It's a rack. Everything hangs from it. Reach for that blue sky-rack. Suddenly, everything fits, everything's solved.

STEARNS (*Indignantly*) What is it? It sounds like a fairy tale, a magic lamp, just another lousy romantic idea.

HALLIDAY No. Not magic. Inspiration! It happened to me a dozen times in a dozen hotel rooms.

STEARNS Bunk!

HALLIDAY How would you know? It wasn't only me—it happened to all of us. We were the generation of the blue sky-rack.

STEARNS I'm fed up to here with your generation. So you had talent, you and a few others. That doesn't make a generation of geniuses. No wonder the whole thing came down on your heads. Your age was bankrupt from the start.

HALLIDAY (*Gradually self-hypnotic*) Bankrupt! Why in one year, nineteen twenty-five, we published Theodore Dreiser's *An American Tragedy,* Sinclair Lewis' *Arrowsmith,* John

Dos Passos' *Manhattan Transfer,* and *The Great Gatsby*. We had luminous books by Glasgow, Cather and Wharton. The unique beginnings of Hemingway, Faulkner, Eliot, Cummings. And it wasn't only our serious stuff. It was an age of wit and brilliant laughter. We had Bob Benchley, Ring Lardner, Dottie Parker and Archy and Mehitabel. Our athletes—Jack Dempsey, the Babe, Red Grange. Big Bill Tilden—it was the Golden Age. Yes, and our stage was alive. Bankrupt? We had O'Neill, George Kelly, Don Stewart, Eddie Justus Mayer. And we had actresses! We were all in love with our stars—maybe that made the difference. We knew how to give them the feeling they were grander than anyone had ever been before. I don't know, maybe I'm just getting to be old and crotchety, but it seems to me our magazines were better, the *Mercury* and *Vanity Fair,* and the *New Yorker* was fresher and more alive. And our songs—why were our songs so much better? "Ain't Misbehavin'" and "My Man" and "Who"—I'll never forget the first time I heard Marilyn Miller sing it—and the *Garrick Gaieties:* "Now tell me what street compares with Mott Street in July?" . . . You don't have anyone who twinkled like Marilyn Miller, haunted you like Jeanne Eagels — I even think our movie stars were better. Valentino was so much more what he was than any of yours today, and Doug had more energy, and Pickford and Gish were more wistful, and Barbara LaMarr and Swanson were more stunning and Carmel Myers was wickeder and Clara Bow was wilder and Alice Joyce and Billie Dove had that breath-taking beauty you don't see any more. And we had Lindy. God how we loved Lindy! Coming out of nowhere and going into everywhere—a living symbol of the blue sky-rack.

STEARNS (*Quietly, still somewhat under the spell*) Boy, you almost had me ... Billie Dove, "Ain't Misbehavin'," all those writers in one year—you make it sound like all the joys, the pure, untroubled joys we Depression kids were cheated out of. (*Raising his voice*) But Lindbergh! You can have your Lindbergh. We give him back to you!

HALLIDAY   There's the difference. Your Lindbergh is the bitter recluse, the political appeaser, the *Luftwaffe* apologist. Our Lindy was the blue-eyed boy, the Lone Eagle, Horatio Alger in an airship conquering space. No politics. Pure heroism and romance.

STEARNS (*With fervor*)   Pure bunkola! You weren't only romantic about Lindbergh, you were romantic about youth— what were your celebrated sheiks and flappers but a bunch of feather-brained kids writing slogans on old Fords? You were romantic about your writers—art for art's sake, above the battle, let's pull the wool over each other's eyes and go to bed. What a party! You were even romantic about the stock market!

HALLIDAY   We had a war to end wars. We saw how hollow that was, so we had a party to end parties.

STEARNS (*Angrily*)   And boy, you did it! You left us to clean up the mess—breadlines and small civil wars between strikers and state police, and young writers so busy starving and picketing for writers' projects that they had no time to write.

HALLIDAY (*Impassioned*)   There's always an excuse, isn't there?

If you're a writer, you find time to write, you make the time, invent the time, create a new clock with a bigger day and longer hours. Your boys weren't writers—they were politicos, junior Lenins. Our fellows had to write. They were writers. They would've written in jail—all they'd ask for was a pencil.

STEARNS Is that the most important thing? Writing? Just writing? What about pain and misery and social injustice?

HALLIDAY That's the mistake your thirties generation makes—separating the two. Writing, art, music is a luxury. When the going gets tough you've got to get rid of the arts—unless they're a weapon in the class struggle— Oh, I've read your pamphlets. Art is superfluous, inconsequential. But art isn't—because it's man looking at himself naked, knowing mankind, telling men a thousand truths, bringing them face to face with the issues that life itself poses, with all its mysteriousness and all its wretched beauty.

STEARNS Champagne and circuses! You starve people and there isn't any art, there isn't any humanity, there isn't any *Friends and Foes*. There isn't any "What street compares with Mott Street . . ." What do you think there've been revolutions for? Those people love art, but they're hungry, goddamn it, and they're not going to appreciate life's sweet mysteries of love until their bellies are full. You jazz-age guys never understood that and that's why the world's in a mess now, a real, sorry mess. And we're in a mess now. You and me. You and I, or whatever the hell the grammar is. Talking about the twenties, pulling the twenties around you like a racoon coat when we're supposed to be pulling a movie together—you're driving me nuts! (*He breaks off, frustrated*) I need a belt! (*He walks decisively to his overnight bag, takes out a pint bottle of whiskey and pours a drink*) I promised myself I wasn't going to drink during working hours, but I feel the moment has come! My girl put this in for luck. Hah!

HALLIDAY (*Silently watching him drink*)   I think you've put your finger on the tragedy—what is man's true interest? The whole consort of one's being trying and trying, or a fraction of one's being writing a movie?

STEARNS (*Striding toward* HALLIDAY)   You know something? At this stage of the game I don't care! That's your answer. If a hood has a gun pointed at your head, you don't speculate. That's your answer. We have a gun pointed at our heads and I'm sick to death of not doing something about it. That damned novel is burning a hole in your pocket and I don't care any more, I'm beginning to doubt you've got anything there.

HALLIDAY (*Shocked*)   What?

STEARNS   Oh, sure, you've got words down, but I don't think you know the score any more and I'm fed up—

HALLIDAY (*Furiously*)   Why, you—young—young—(*The telephone rings as they stand face to face, fists clenched.* HALLIDAY's *voice falls off to a whisper*) . . . young . . .

STEARNS (*Answering the phone*) Yes!... No, he hasn't come back yet. I don't know where he is.
(*He hangs up*)

HALLIDAY (*Subdued*) Thanks.

STEARNS And I wish she'd stop calling. I'm not a good liar.

HALLIDAY I know what you're thinking—Lindy outlived his time and so did Manley Halliday.

STEARNS (*His voice rising again*) You're right! You're exactly right, Mr. Halliday.

HALLIDAY Well, you're wrong. You're exactly wrong, Mr. Stearns. They told me that once in Positano and I showed them—

STEARNS (*Furiously*) You're all coked up with dreams of past glory. Once in Positano! Once upon a time!

HALLIDAY (*With a touch of desperation*) I'm not talking once upon a time. I'm talking right now. What I've got in my pocket—

STEARNS You write a novel? You can't even write a lousy movie script! You're all talk now.

HALLIDAY   All right, Shep! Okay, Shep. No dreams, no talk. I'll show you! (*He slowly reaches for his manuscript in his inside jacket pocket and painfully holds it out to* STEARNS) Now, you go ahead and read that. If it doesn't say something to your new, Depression-proud, cocksure generation—if it doesn't say anything—I mean it, if it doesn't—I'll tear it up. You be the judge—you yourself. (STEARNS *hesitatingly reaches with both hands for the manuscript.* HALLIDAY, *with difficulty, finally lets go. He holds his hands as though they had lost something precious, as* STEARNS *turns with concern toward the typewriter and their unfinished movie outline.* HALLIDAY *stops him*) You read. I'll write . . . And don't worry—the blue sky-rack. (*He walks to the typewriter as* STEARNS, *reading slowly, moves to the bedroom door.* HALLIDAY *begins to muse aloud, a preliminary to work, as* STEARNS *exits*) Ski captain . . . waitress . . . Put them through what I know . . . throw them into my whole sad, funny world . . . (*The past begins to creep into the room. Music is heard, and a song is being sung, all from another room; the songs suggest the late nineteen twenties; lights change and Japanese lanterns are lowered as part of the decoration for an elaborate Hollywood party. The Waldorf sitting room becomes a drawing room, beyond which a moonlit swimming pool is visible*) . . . my whole funny, sad world . . .

> (*Party guests are drifting into the room as* HALLIDAY, *once again, becomes transformed into a younger, handsomer, gayer man, not through a change in clothes, but through his style and manner*)

FREDDY (*A successful movie director with an English accent*) Aren't you Hallidays marvelous! Here you are, giving this wonderful party for Rin-Tin-Tin's stand-in while bankers can't think of anything to do about the crash except jump out of hotel windows.

GEORGETTE (*A vivacious starlet*) Parties raise morale and circulate money. Maybe more parties will solve the whole thing.

HALLIDAY (*Showing the effects of alcohol, but self-confident*) Georgette, you may have the new Herbert Hoover slogan: A chicken in every pot and a party in every patio.

MAN (*A cigar-smoking casting director*) It must be marvelous to have so many famous friends come to your party. How do you do it?

HALLIDAY It's very simple. When these friends arrive and I don't know them, I introduce myself.
    (*He shakes hands with the man, introducing himself. They all laugh*)

GIRL That's Victor Milgrim!

GEORGETTE Who he?

FREDDY Just the youngest genius in Hollywood.

HALLIDAY This year.

MILGRIM There you are, Manley. Beautiful party, Halliday. I suppose it's no use trying to lure you into doing a picture for me?

(*The guests stroll out toward the music*)

HALLIDAY   Pictures—what are they?

MILGRIM (*Chuckling*)   Just our blood . . . Not even if I signed the check and let you fill in the amount?

HALLIDAY   I'd write it for ten million, I'd buy the studio and close it down.

MILGRIM (*Lightly*)   Forget I mentioned it.

JERE (*Entering, but still talking in a frenetic and gay mood to invisible people in the next room. She wears a stunning gown of the period, and elaborate jewelry*)   Larry, you parlor snake! The moment I turn my back, you start necking with your wife. I knew you were cheating on me.

MILGRIM (*Turning to her*)   Mrs. Halliday, can't you prevail on your husband to give me a few months of his time for a small fortune?

JERE   I'd never let him work for the movies. He's too talented.

MILGRIM   Well, it's a beautiful party.
(*He exits with a girl who has been waiting for him*)

HALLIDAY (*Grimly*)   I've been looking for you all evening.

JERE   No, you've been avoiding me all evening. I smiled at you across the room and you turned away. I'm Jere Halliday. Didn't we meet in Paris on Armistice night?

HALLIDAY   You or somebody—probably somebody—ordered six additional cases of champagne. That's seven hundred more dollars we don't have.

JERE   You're spoiling our party with statistics. Champagne, it's naturally expensive. What happened to the money we had last week?

HALLIDAY (*He reaches for her necklace and jerks it off*)   You're wearing it tonight.

JERE   You're spoiling our party. If we have to talk about things, let's do it after the party.
(*She begins to sob*)

HALLIDAY   One of these days there won't be any after the party. You never used to cry. Are you crying because you're drinking or drinking because you're crying?

JERE (*Violently*)   Stop analyzing me! Will people never stop analyzing me? First that horrible doctor in Vienna you made me go to.

HALLIDAY   He was doing you some good. You should've stayed.

JERE   He was an old goat with lascivious fingers. I hated him!

HALLIDAY   It was the truth you hated. You're lying to yourself.
For months I've been trying to get you to help me draw up
our balance sheet. Not just our finances, but of our lives,
where we're going, what we're doing to each other. Oh, Jere,
Jere, let's not get stuck in this tunnel of lovelessness.
   (WISTER LA SALLE *enters. He is a famous Hollywood sing-*
   ing star, traditionally handsome)

LA SALLE   How drab! Making love to your own wife!

JERE (*Going to* LA SALLE)   Wister, how clever of you to come for
me at this moment.

LA SALLE   How are you, Halliday? (*To* JERE)   I've been search-
ing this windy stable for you—you dissipated choir boy.

JERE   Oh, Wister, you're heaven.
   (*As* LA SALLE *is about to leave with* JERE, BORIS SHLEPNIKOV
   enters, as do a number of the party guests, and this stops
   the departing couple. There is subdued merriment and
   furtive exchanges of anticipation among the guests. BORIS
   is a small man, immaculately dressed, with decorations
   and ribbons and a beard of Czarist vintage)

BORIS (*With a marked Russian accent*)   Mr. Halliday, may I present myself—I am Boris Ilyitch Shlepnikov. No doubt you have seen some of my famous sculptures.

HALLIDAY (*Preoccupied*) Yes, yes . . . I guess so.

BORIS I have done some of the most famous beauties in the nude, lovely creatures all.

HALLIDAY (*Absently*) Interesting work.

BORIS But my most beautiful models cannot compare to the ravishing Mrs. Halliday.
(*He gestures toward her and* JERE *curtsies*)

HALLIDAY Thank you.

BORIS The red-gold hair of a Degas beauty. Eyes that would turn the meekest of men into Casanovas. Shoulders that plead for caresses.

HALLIDAY Now, look!

BORIS In the name of art, you must permit your wife to come to my studio in Carmel for one glorious week.

HALLIDAY (*Incensed*) Not for one day!

BORIS Your charming wife has already agreed.

HALLIDAY Jere!

BORIS To sculpt the human body, I must know that body—search out its most delicious secrets—

HALLIDAY Why, you son of a bitch!
(*He violently grabs* BORIS *and hurls him against a chair*)

BORIS (*Alarmed*) Hold it, Mr. Halliday, don't you know who I am?

JERE Mannie!

FREDDY (*Pulling* HALLIDAY *off* BORIS) It's only a joke. It's Gus Jones!

BORIS (*Pulling off his fake beard and speaking in his natural American tongue*) Yeah, Mr. Halliday. Your wife hired me to rib the guests. I just pulled it on Doug about Mary and he thought it was a howl.

HALLIDAY (*After a pause, he smooths down the lapels of* BORIS' *jacket*) I think it's sadistic. You're fired.

JERE Mannie!
(BORIS *exits rapidly as the other guests leave with varying degrees of surprise and disappointment and even mocking laughter.* JERE *tries to communicate with* HALLIDAY *but he turns away coldly*)

LA SALLE (*To* JERE)   Our fans are clamoring for us. What shall we sing?

JERE (*Desperately gay*)   A duet from *La Bohème?*

LA SALLE   By Fats Waller!
(*He jazzes up Puccini as they exit. Now that the room is cleared,* HALLIDAY *sees* SEIXAS, *who has entered unobtrusively during the* SHLEPNIKOV *incident*)

HALLIDAY   Burt! What are you doing in this madhouse?

SEIXAS   Manley, we were supposed to meet tonight.

HALLIDAY   Forgot about this party. Forgot everything. Shouldn't've forgot you. Y'know, I love you, Burt. (*Pours himself a drink*) Have a drink.

SEIXAS   No, thanks. We don't have much to say to each other, do we?

HALLIDAY   Whatever it is, though, this is a hell of a place to say it . . .

SEIXAS   Manley, it's the first time we have to say no.

HALLIDAY   I'm over the hump, Burt. Got the novel practically finished, broken its back.

SEIXAS   You were over the hump three years ago. Manley, the firm is fed up.

HALLIDAY   They're crazy! *Folly and Farewell* is a good novel, best I've ever done maybe, most personal true story of me, Jere, you—whole sad, funny world.

SEIXAS   I've run out of ammunition. And now with the crash— it's impossible. Just look at this crazy house. How the devil could even a hack writer work here?

HALLIDAY   Burt, I've lost the gift, the knack, for clearing the decks.

SEIXAS   Manley, break away! Take Jere and go somewhere. Don't tell anybody, tear out the telephone, and work!

HALLIDAY   My will power, my bank account, my marriage, my work—need work! What a panic it's been!
        (*The sounds of music and drunken laughter from the next room grow louder*)

SEIXAS   You've got your talent. That bank hasn't gone under yet, and never will. Just change this terrible, terrible life—
        (*Guests spill into the room and begin to chase each other as they shriek and laugh drunkenly*)

MAN   Come on, Hallie boy, we're going to play water polo.

63

ACTRESS   One team with their clothes on—

MAN   The other with their clothes off.
   (*They start to remove bits of their clothing as they dash toward the pool*)

SEIXAS   I've got to get out of here!
   (*He leaves abruptly as* JERE *and* LA SALLE *run through the room in pursuit of the disrobing guests.* HALLIDAY *steps between them, forcing* JERE *to remain as* LA SALLE *departs*)

HALLIDAY   (*Drinking*)   Jere, what do you see in an ass like Wister-dear?

JERE   I see a silly handsome darling with a golden voice.
   (*She starts off. He blocks her way*)

HALLIDAY   A golden ass!... Jere, I love you.

JERE   It's not fun any more, Mannie.

HALLIDAY   For God's sake, we're older! We've got a six-year-old boy. You're not content to drink from the fountain of youth. You keep leaning over to see your own image. And you keep falling in. You're drowning.

JERE   I'm not leaning over to see myself. I'm trying to fish you out.

HALLIDAY   Well, you don't have to bother fishing me out any more. There's no water in the fountain. No youth. Here's the oldest fact in the world. We're broke.

JERE   Oh, Mannie, I hate the grubbing around ... What about Seixas?

HALLIDAY   He turned me down. No more advances. Advances *fini!* Advances *kaput!*

JERE   How could he?

HALLIDAY   (*Anguished*)   Christ, you know how he could. You know the worst part of my session with Burt? He didn't ask to see it ... the novel ... even if it wasn't finished. He never asked to see it. And you never asked to see it! Used to hang on my shoulder. Used to love to watch me work. Not any more! You never looked at this one. Why? (*He takes hold of her arm fiercely*) Too damn busy! Too damn many buddies!

JERE   They're not my buddies! Your buddies. Tell them to leave me alone—

HALLIDAY   Just the last page! About us. The whole truth about us. The intimate, intricate, inanimate truth about us. Read it. Pat it on the head like a dog. Wait right here. Don't move! Be right back.

> (*He exits, weaving drunkenly.* JERE, *alone for the first time, gives way to tears of love, depression and confusion. As the amorous* LA SALLE *enters, she regains control of*

herself and becomes once again the brittle, gay party girl.
He chases her briefly, forcing her into a chair)

LA SALLE My gaiety is a mask. I'm nearly out of my mind.
You're adorable, beautiful!! I've a marvelous hideaway. From
the window by my bed you can see the whole city spread at
your feet like jewels on black velvet.

JERE Will you make me feel aquamarine?

LA SALLE The whole spectrum! Choose your color.

JERE And later, Venetian red?

LA SALLE I give you the rainbow!

JERE I might go! I don't feel any colors here any more. (*He
kisses her, lifts her in his arms and carries her to the door*)
Oh, no! Put me down! I'll have to tell Manley.

LA SALLE Oh, no you don't! I don't like it *that* sophisticated. Off
you go!

JERE I couldn't. I never ran away from Manley before. Never.
I must, must tell him.

LA SALLE No! It isn't done. It's absurd. It's—it's impossible.
(HALLIDAY *enters quietly, manuscript in hand*)

66

JERE   Then I won't go!

LA SALLE   All right, but hurry. I'll be waiting outside.
(*He kisses her shoulder and departs*)

HALLIDAY (*After a long silence*)   That was fascinating. What
are you waiting for? Go, bitch! Go on. Have your night!
(*From a distance the tinkling gay music of "Ain't We
Got Fun" is heard*)

JERE   Mannie, help me. I'm breaking into a thousand pieces and
only you can put me together again.

HALLIDAY   I tried putting you together—now let the Wister La
Salles try . . . let all the king's horses and all the king's men!

JERE (*Reaching out her arms to him*)   I don't want to go. I
love you, Manley. Tell me not to go, Manley. Tell me not to
go! I need you to tell me . . . (*Pleading*) Tell me no and I
won't go. I love you, Mannie. Tell me no.

HALLIDAY (*In mounting frenzy*)   I tell you—yes. Yes! Yes! *Yes!*
(*She gasps and rushes out. For a moment* HALLIDAY *stands
dazed and forlorn and then the party engulfs him*)

FREDDY   Here's Manley . . . You must see this, *mon ami*—a
scene from my next picture . . .
(*The party now becomes frenzied. Everyone is shouting
and shrieking at the same time*)

BORIS   One more won't hurt you.

ACTRESS   What a marvelous party.

FREDDY   Great, just the greatest thing since the ten commandments!

BORIS   Which one, God's or De Mille's?

FREDDY   Better not let C.B. hear you give him second billing.

GEORGETTE   Pardon me while I go into my strange innertube.

ACTOR   She's a Hoover girl. She just lies down and lets it happen to her.

MAN   Oh, Christ! Every time she has four or five drinks she has to get up and dance.

ACTRESS   I wish she'd just faw down and go boom.

GEORGETTE   I think Manley Halliday is the cat's pajamas!

HALLIDAY (*With sudden violence*)   Party is over! I said it's over. Everybody the hell out! (*The guests stand dazed with surprise. He begins to throw them out physically. He is in a maniacal rage and the guests flee in terror*) Goddamn out. Goddamn them. Out. Over. Finished. *Fini. Kaput* . . . (*In quiet despair*) Jere ... you couldn't. Not with La Salle. With nobody. With nobody! (*With his last phrase, which is wrenched from his throat, he finds that he has torn his manuscript in two. Stunned, as though he has torn himself in two, he sinks into a chair. With drunken deliberation he begins to tear the torn manuscript into strips. When he completes this act of destruction, he cradles the shredded manuscript to him. Tenderly, he carries it to just behind the door and dumps it in a heap on the floor. In the darkening room, he finds a match, strikes it and sets the manuscript on fire*) Burn, damn you, burn. (*He slams the door shut and leans against it. As the past, with its moonlit swimming pool and lanterns, begins to grow dim, flames and smoke appear*) Oh, Jere! Jere! How do we get out of this amusement park?

(*Now the past has faded out completely and we are back in the present, in the Waldorf. A knock is heard and* STEARNS, *entering from the bedroom, goes to the door*)

MILGRIM (*Entering briskly*)   Well, how are you two geniuses getting along? I like the way the room looks—worked in, a healthy disorder. I expect nothing short of a masterpiece. Is that it? Looks like you've got the screen play all done.

STEARNS (*Still holding* HALLIDAY's *novel*)   No, this is something else.

MILGRIM   You're not reading someone else's story on my time? (*He laughs disarmingly*)

STEARNS   No, we've been working steadily.

MILGRIM   Good, I can't wait to hear the new attack on the story. I'd like to hear it now and then we'll huddle again when I get back from the theatre.

HALLIDAY (*Still somewhat dazed*)   Victor . . .

STEARNS   Mr. Milgrim, we haven't quite finished putting it down on paper yet.

MILGRIM   Nothing on paper? Well—I told you what a pressure-bind we're in. What have you been doing for three days?

HALLIDAY   Has it only been three days?

STEARNS   We thought we'd run over our story line a few more times and then sit down and bang it out tonight.

MILGRIM   Why does it always have to be the last minute? Why are writers congenitally unable to write until their heads are on the guillotine block?

HALLIDAY   All we need is another couple of hours.

STEARNS   We could *read* it to you then.

MILGRIM   No, I'd rather hear whatever you've got right now. In the morning there'll be a second-unit crew at Webster costing me four thousand a day. Now let's get down to business. I've flown three thousand miles to hear this story. Go ahead, Manley.

HALLIDAY   Victor, I think it's only fair that we tell you—

STEARNS (*Interrupting anxiously*)   You see, Mr. Milgrim, we have this ski captain. He's a real, honest all-American boy who gets mixed up with a gang from New York—

HALLIDAY   Nize, baby, et opp all da screen play.

MILGRIM   What did you say, Manley?

HALLIDAY   Victor, we don't have a story. We don't have any story at all.

MILGRIM (*Striding to* HALLIDAY)   What *have* you been doing? (*Noticing* STEARNS' *whiskey bottle*) Hitting this?

HALLIDAY   Victor, we've had one hell of a time getting acquainted. A collaboration is like a marriage—

MILGRIM (*Breaking in angrily*)   Dammit, don't give me any of your highbrow analogies!

STEARNS   Mr. Milgrim, we keep looking for something better.

MILGRIM   Look, gentlemen, I'm a perfectionist myself, up to a point. Then I become a realist. Now what are the realities? I'm paying you, Manley, two thousand dollars a week. I'm paying you, Stearns, the maximum junior writer's salary. And what have I got to show for it? (*He snatches up the wastebasket and dumps its contents on the floor*) Crumpled paper, perfection! I don't want a wastebasket full of perfection. What I want—and what I intend to get—is a coherent, detailed shooting outline that I can put in the hands of my director in the morning. And that you can present to the dean and his staff at five o'clock tomorrow afternoon. Stay up all night if you have to. Take Benzedrine if you need it. Only don't fail me. I'm warning you, Manley—both of you—you better not fail me. We're all committed now, we're locked together. (*He goes to the door*) It's been snowing at Webster all day. The weather is perfect for winter sports and photography. All the elements are ready, you be ready too. Ah . . . (*He tries to remember if he has omitted anything*) Good night, gentlemen.

    (*He exits*)

STEARNS (*After a pained silence*)   I feel like I've been taken behind the woodshed and given an old-fashioned whipping.

HALLIDAY   Stearns, Victor was talking for an industry that is set up to grind out a dream a day—and grind it must. Even though it grinds with it the flesh and bones and dignity of hirelings like us. In my case a temporary hireling.

STEARNS   Manley, if you ever got the blue sky-rack, get it now.

HALLIDAY (*Holding an imaginary glass*)   To the blue sky-rack.

STEARNS   To buckets of Benzedrine and the blue sky-rack.

HALLIDAY (*He types a few lines and then reads*)   *Love on Ice,*
by Manley Halliday and Shep Stearns. Sound all right to you?

STEARNS   Sounds great. That's a good start. (*A knock on the
door is heard*) It's Victor again—the Waldorf's own Benzedrine pusher.
   (*As* HALLIDAY *goes to the door,* STEARNS *rushes to the typewriter and simulates a man hard at work.* HALLIDAY *opens
   the door*)

HALLIDAY (*Shocked*)   Jere!
   (*The real present-day* JERE *enters. Her figure has thick-
   ened, her make-up is overdone. She is a macabre, middle-
   aged version of the enthralling, younger* JERE)

JERE (*Straining for the old gaiety*)   I'm Hilda von Hulings-
chaft, Operator Four-eight-six, and I've finally tracked you to
your lair.

HALLIDAY (*Flatly*)   Jere! Come in. Meet Shep Stearns, my collaborator. Shep, this is Mrs. Halliday.

JERE   Let me look at you . . . I never thought of you as ever
getting gray.

HALLIDAY   I know.

JERE   How do you do, Mr. Stearns. *Enchanté.*

STEARNS (*Nervously*)   How do you do, Mrs. Halliday? Would you excuse me? Got a lot of work to do. (*He starts to go, then stops and confronts* JERE *with decision*) Mrs. Halliday, could you possibly see Manley on his way back? We have a murderous deadline. We need every minute now.

JERE   One minute and I'll disappear like a pumpkin coach.

HALLIDAY   It's all right, Shep. We won't be long.
       (STEARNS *exits, taking* HALLIDAY'S *manuscript into the bedroom with him*)

JERE   Ah, the young are getting so much younger . . . (*She waits for* HALLIDAY *to help her off with her coat. He hesitates, wanting to keep his distance, then complies*) I had to come to see you . . . I always have to follow my impulses when I feel mauve.

HALLIDAY   I feel gray around the gills. I've got a producer on my back. All the clocks are running.

JERE   What in the world are you writing—the *Ice Follies?* I can't imagine you writing for the movies.

HALLIDAY   Neither can I.

JERE   Oh, by the way, I win the fur-lined cuspidor. It looks like New Directions is going to publish my Rimbaud.

HALLIDAY   Good. They're doing nice things.

JERE   I just have to sharpen "*Adieu*" and—(*She notices the bottle of whiskey*)—change a few words in "*Faim*."

HALLIDAY   Good.

JERE   Mannie, I know what you're going to say, but we really get the most amazing results with AA.

HALLIDAY   Look, Jere, I don't need AA. I haven't had a drink in almost a year now.

JERE   But, Mannie, darling, once you take the step, it's such a satisfaction.

HALLIDAY   I don't want to spend the rest of **my** life nursing drunks. I've got to *work*. I've lost so much time.

JERE   Manley, if you could see yourself. You look ghastly.
(*She attempts to straighten his tie but he moves away*)

HALLIDAY   I don't care how I *look* any more.

JERE   But, Mannie, there's a difference between being casual and being sloppy.

HALLIDAY   Surely you didn't come up here just to make that distinction.

JERE (*Sitting down*)   All right, Mannie, I guess I am getting to be an old spinster bitch. Who have you seen lately—of the old crowd?

HALLIDAY   I don't see anybody any more.

JERE   Phil?

HALLIDAY   In his second childhood. B scenarios and extra girls.

JERE   Harold?

HALLIDAY   At Romanoff's every night, half potted, playing gin with his agent until closing time.

JERE   *Sic transit*—

HALLIDAY   Not *gloria*. Promises.

JERE (*After a short awkward pause*)   Mannie, I hate to bring up the horrid subject of money the first time I see you in years. But there's all that back alimony—

HALLIDAY   I sent you some money three days ago.

JERE   Yes, but it wasn't that much. It didn't last me a day.

HALLIDAY   It was half my check—a thousand dollars!

JERE But I was two months behind in my rent—that was six hundred right there—

HALLIDAY I wrote you years ago that you couldn't afford your apartment any more. I'm not made of gold. I can't keep you in the style of a—

JERE I've got all our lovely things there. I'd just die if I had to leave it. Besides, it isn't only me. It's a place for Douglas to come home to from school. And, Mannie, that's the main reason I came. Do you know what you've done?

HALLIDAY What else have I done?

JERE Your son has left school.

HALLIDAY What on earth for?

JERE How would you feel if the bursar called you in every few weeks and asked why your father hasn't paid your tuition?

HALLIDAY I airmailed it. It's the first thing I did after I got my check.

JERE Well, it was too late. He'd run away from school before that. He came home sobbing because he didn't have enough money to invite a girl to the junior prom.

HALLIDAY I want to see him through that school— God, Jere, give me a chance. The only reason I'm doing this damn movie is to meet my responsibilities. But you've got to help too. Douglas has to learn that he's not the son of a millionaire and no matter how many extravagant mementos you have in that apartment, you've got to throw them out, and you've got to move, you've simply got—(JERE *takes a handkerchief from her bag and dabs at her eyes*) Jere, Jere, don't cry. Please don't cry.

JERE (*With an effort at light-heartedness*) Look at me—leaking like an old hose ... (*He walks over to console her, then stops just short of touching her. Desperately, she clutches his hand with both of hers*) Oh, Mannie, Mannie, I'm sorry but it's being so goddamn alone. God Almighty, the nights I haven't been able to sleep, thinking about it. Tracing it back. Where, where was it that it happened? It drives me crazy. (*Gently, he manages to withdraw his hand and then moves a few steps away from her. She quickly follows*) How many times I've been at the phone to call you. I just drag along, existing without you. I'm sure my maid thinks I'm a lunatic because once in a while I forget and she hears me talking to you ... Mannie, we're both getting older. We're more sensible now. We don't drink any more— After all, that was the main trouble, wasn't it? And it would be so good for Douglas. Don't you think if we both worked at it as a full-time thing—

HALLIDAY Jere, I simply haven't the time or strength to go through all this with you again.

JERE I know it isn't going to be easy for either of us. We'll never solve our problems by running away from them. Mannie, you have to learn to face yourself.

HALLIDAY (*Wearily*) Jere, don't start lecturing me again. I'm in no mood for lectures these days.

JERE I believe I know what's best for both of us, I've learned to make sacrifices—they're good for the soul.

HALLIDAY (*In mounting anger*) Jere, for God's sake, leave my soul alone.

JERE (*Her voice rising sharply*) I know why you're against it, because I'm for it. You always were against everything I tried to do. You told me I'd never finish my translation. But in spite of your jealousy, I am finishing it!

HALLIDAY Must you dig up all those old fights over again?

JERE You were the one who started to . . .

HALLIDAY Why can't we agree that it's dead between us, that we stifle each other—

JERE (*Shouting*) Will you let me finish! You never let me finish!

HALLIDAY Finish? You never let yourself finish! If you had your way you'd talk me deaf, dumb and blind until doomsday.

    (*She slaps him hard across his face. He turns away from her*)

JERE (*Reaching out for him*) I love you, Mannie. Why does it always happen like this?

HALLIDAY (*Desperately*) Get out of here! I'll send you your money. But stay away from me. Leave me alone.

JERE (*Patiently*) One of these days you'll want me back. And I'll come back. (STEARNS *enters. She goes to the door and turns to* HALLIDAY *lovingly*) I know us so well now.
(*She exits.* HALLIDAY *stands with his head bowed as* STEARNS *watches him. Their eyes meet. They stare at each other for a long moment*)

HALLIDAY Stearns, I wonder if a man can ever really love a woman without hating her too. Like the shipwrecked mariner, the rock on which I founder is the rock to which I cling.
(*Fighting to control his anguish, he exits into the bedroom*)

STEARNS (*After a moment of listening, he rushes to the telephone*) Get me University nine, one-five-five-five—Mr. Seixas, this is Shep Stearns. I've got to be quick. I've been reading *Folly and Farewell*. I know all his books—but this one—this one is so much more—you've got to read it right away because he may turn against it and tear it up. Mrs. Halliday was just here. He's coming! I'll leave it at the desk.
(*He hangs up sharply*)

HALLIDAY (*Entering with an air of determination*) This night belongs to Victor Milgrim.

STEARNS   To the victor belongs the detailed shooting outline!
(*He pours a drink and raises it in a toast*) To our hero, the
intrepid ski captain, who is either rich, proud and snobbish,
or poor and working his way through college or—or whatever
the hell else we'll think up on the train!
   (*He drinks.* HALLIDAY *raises an imaginary glass*)

HALLIDAY (*Toasting*)   To our heroine, who is either a buxom
red-headed waitress in a hash joint, or a bony *Harper's Bazaar*
model—or a fantastic combination of both.

STEARNS (*Laughing, his spirits soaring*)   Tonight the blue sky-
rack. Tomorrow Webster! We're off to the frozen North.
Mush!
   (*He sits down to work*)

HALLIDAY (*Quietly, painfully*)   That's what we've got to write
—mush!
   (*He stares at his empty hand for a long moment, then
   stares at the bottle on the table for a moment. Suddenly,
   almost involuntarily, he pours himself a drink, hesitates
   for a split second, then convulsively gulps the drink down
   as* STEARNS, *shocked and fearful, slowly rises*)

Curtain

ACT THREE

The next day, Saturday, late afternoon, a sparsely furnished attic room at Webster Inn. HALLIDAY, *unshaven and somewhat drunk, is resting on the chaise while* STEARNS *is trying to work. An empty whiskey bottle and a half-full one are in evidence. "God Rest Ye Merry, Gentlemen," played on chimes, is heard in the room.*

HALLIDAY (*Thickly*) Playing a melody on the chimes makes me think of a man picking out a tune on the piano with his feet.

STEARNS What if the professional model doesn't win— The waitress—

HALLIDAY Lord, I'm sick of that waitress! I thought we'd left her on the train. Not my feet though. Feet fell off in the snow. (*He stands with difficulty*) Got a better idea. We keep the model. Here's the twist. She has a baby. So when the ice she's standing on begins to carry her away from the bank ... (*He breaks off in disgust*) Aaaaah! Nize, baby, et up all the ize.
(*The chimes strike four*)

STEARNS (*Distraught*) Ten minutes ago it was three o'clock.
(MILGRIM *enters without knocking*)

HALLIDAY Sit down, Victor, pull up a bed.

MILGRIM My second-unit crew is standing around throwing snowballs at each other. Expensive fun ... How did you get up here? I wanted you right across the hall from me.

HALLIDAY You ought to tighten up your infield, Victor. When we got to the desk, no reservations—no room at the Inn.

MILGRIM Why didn't you call me?

HALLIDAY I like it here. Symbol of writer's status in Hollywood.

MILGRIM It looks more like a symbol of contractual irresponsibility to me. You promised me a story. Your agent gave me your word you'd stay sober on this job.

HALLIDAY You'll get your story! Victor, I finished *Shadow Ball* in Presbyterian Hospital, but I finished it. This mountain can be climbed!
  (*He bangs his drained whiskey glass on the table*)

MILGRIM Stearns, you find the director. He's pacing the lobby. If you have anything—or can think something up on the way —give it to him. And then come back on the double.

STEARNS (*Starts to leave; then, noticing that* HALLIDAY *is in pain, goes toward him*) Stay with it, baby.

MILGRIM (*Shouting*) We're counting minutes now! (STEARNS *exits hurriedly*) It's inconceivable that you haven't found a story. This place is teeming with fresh ideas. I've talked to a dozen kids here and each one is a whole screen play. (*He sits down facing* HALLIDAY) You've got to find a story for them—and it must reflect credit on Webster.

HALLIDAY (*Pointing at* MILGRIM's *eyes*)   Victor, I see a hunger in your eyes. Victor Milgrim, you want a badge of honor from the Halls of Ivy!

MILGRIM   My only diploma was from Congress High in Bridgeport and I worked nights taking tickets in a movie house. What's wrong with wanting an honorary degree from Webster?

HALLIDAY   There's nothing wrong with *what!* It's *how!*

MILGRIM   I'm not interested in your philosophy! I need you and you need me. Whether we like it or not, we're tied to-gether.
(*He takes up the whiskey bottle as he starts to go*)

HALLIDAY   Victor?
(*He holds his hands out for the bottle*)

MILGRIM (*Tossing it to him*)   Be ready at five.
(*He exits*)

STEARNS (*Entering a moment later, watching* MILGRIM *depart*)   God, it stinks in here—booze and tobacco . . . (*He starts to change his shirt*) Funny, ever since they sprung me out of here five years ago, I've had dreams how I'd come back in style. Showing up with someone like you or Hemingway. And now it's just something to go through, to get over with as painlessly as possible.

HALLIDAY   That isn't funny. That's the big practical joke of growing up. After a while you don't count the years, you count the number of your disenchantments. You—

STEARNS   Shut up, Manley!

HALLIDAY   Okay, laddie, okay, Shep, okay, okay ... Hell with all this talking. We both sit down and write the script. Which half do you want? You take the first half and I'll take the last. At five minutes to five, we bring the two halves together and we'll drive in a golden spike at the place where they connect.

STEARNS   Manley, you're drunk. You're cockeyed drunk.

HALLIDAY   No, I'm not drunk. Not only drunk. I'm sick. My heart's filled with tobacco juice. Write both halves myself. Never give up, kid. Remember that.

STEARNS   You know the best thing you can do? Just nod and smile and look famous. Here's a fresh shirt, and, Manley, put your shoes on. In a couple of minutes we're due in Milgrim's suite.

HALLIDAY   (*Putting his shoes on*)   Not going to Milgrim's suite.

STEARNS What?

HALLIDAY Not going to Victor Milgrim's suite.

STEARNS Who was just saying never give up, kid?

HALLIDAY (*Changing his shirt, shakily*) Not giving up. Did you ever see a bullfight? Know what moved me the most? The battered bull—when he stakes out his terrain against the *barrera* and refuses to be lured out. No blandishments, no graceful passes, no seductions, no insults can lure him out! If you want to find me with your sword, *come to me!* Against the *barrera*. Waiting for his moment of truth ... This is our *barrera*.

STEARNS This is a script conference! And it's Milgrim who is saying, Find me with your script. He's waiting for us!

HALLIDAY If I'm going to be a monkey act in Milgrim's circus, let it be in my own cage.

STEARNS Manley, you know what this means to me. It should mean a hell of a lot more to *you*. That novel of yours! You've always known how—

HALLIDAY (*Poignantly*) Haven't you finished it yet? Give it back to me. I need it. I feel unarmed without it.

STEARNS (*Pushing* HALLIDAY *into a chair*) Listen to me, you're not! That book's like a Colt forty-five. It knocks you down . . . I can't give it back to you yet. I gave it to Mr. Seixas.

HALLIDAY (*Playfully tapping* STEARNS' *jaw with a woefully weak fist*) You betrayed me.

STEARNS You've always known what! You've even known how, but now you know why! You showed me why. I'm not even sure you know what a book that is. Mr. Seixas thinks it's the best five and one-half chapters you ever wrote, and so do I.

HALLIDAY (*Puts an affectionate hand on* STEARNS' *shoulder*) Ah, pour it in, pour it in, it's better than insulin, better than blood and glucose.

STEARNS Manley, that's why we've got to go down there! I'd be a monkey on a string, I'd dangle from a chain, I'd use any goddamn means to finish a book like that.

HALLIDAY That's suspect. Use goddamn means to get godly end and godly end could end up damned.

STEARNS That book's got to be finished!

HALLIDAY Tell 'im. Tell 'im the mountain's got to come to Mohammed, because Mohammed can't put one foot before the other—

Jason Robards, Jr., and Rosemary Harris,
as MANLEY and JERE HALLIDAY

STEARNS   Okay, I'll try. Manley, if you need an insulin shot, take it; whatever you need except whiskey, take it.

HALLIDAY   Okay, laddie, okay, okay, okay.

STEARNS   I descend to the first circle of Hell.
   (*He goes*)

HALLIDAY   (*He picks up a pad and pencil and thinks aloud as he is poised to write*)   The fundamental character of everyone, the bottom-dog nature of them, the mixture in them, the strength and weakness in them, the living, loving, eating, pleasing, smoking, drinking, thinking, scolding, working, talking, laughing, dreaming, scheming, worrying, wondering potential and fulfillment.
   (*As he finishes, the past begins to encroach on the present. The drab attic room is transformed into a sun-drenched beach cottage in La Jolla, with the sea shimmering in the distance.* HALLIDAY *is convalescing—the result of the Hollywood party fire*)

JERE   (*Running in radiantly*)   Mannie, look what I found on the beach! A driftwood Brancusi.

HALLIDAY   The sea is Brancusi!

JERE   (*Tenderly*)   I love these two weeks.

HALLIDAY   I haven't been so alive in years. I hear the wind and the gulls, and the sandpipers and, Jere, I even hear the mist. Jere, will you marry me?

JERE   Do you think we know each other well enough?

HALLIDAY   Ever since the fire, I've been thinking about us.

JERE   I'll never run away again.

HALLIDAY   I'm grateful to Wister Whatizname. He brought us back.

JERE   Oh, Mannie, dearest. I don't love you the way I once did.

HALLIDAY   Hm?

JERE   I don't love you wildly any more. I've got that second-wind of love.

HALLIDAY   I'm grateful to that fire. It reduced to ashes our merry-go-round that seemed so dazzling and was really so tawdry.

JERE   That's done now.

HALLIDAY   All done now! I'm going to be a miser of time and count the hours. I've given so many away. Cease to be whirled about.

92

JERE   There isn't anything I lost in the fire that I miss—except —*Folly and Farewell*.

HALLIDAY   I don't even regret that. It wasn't good enough. When I'm ready I'll write it again—only better. A new *Folly and Farewell*.

JERE   That's a wonderful idea! Start it tonight!

HALLIDAY   Before I compose another book, I have to compose myself. I've started to make a list of all my faults. (*He reaches for a pad and reads*) One: vanity. Two: vanity. Three: vanity. All my faults turn out to be the same fault, an over-developed concern to hear my name at the end of the cheers.

JERE (*In a melancholy tone*)   Hurrah for Halliday! Hurrah for Halliday!

HALLIDAY   Hurrah for Baudelaire, who said, "Pleasure consumes us, work resumes us. Let us choose."

JERE   I choose no parties.

HALLIDAY   I choose no friends.

JERE   I choose no bottles.

HALLIDAY   No fifths, no pints, no jiggers.

JERE   I choose us!

HALLIDAY   I choose us, too.

JERE (*She embraces him*)   Oh, Mannie, I love you so much. Will you love me soon?

HALLIDAY   I love you now.

JERE   I mean *make*—love . . . soon?

HALLIDAY   Soon . . . I'll do everything—soon.
  (*The telephone rings. They listen, disturbed*)

JERE (*Finally answering it*)   Hello . . . Bertie? Bertie Bishop . . . no you can't come here! We don't want cold bird and champagne. We're sick. We're quarantined. It's—it's leprosy. If you come here, your fingers will fall off. (*She hangs up*) Mannie, we've got to get out of here! Let's find an island some place.

HALLIDAY   We've got to stop running. We've been to all the islands. That some place is here—right here!
  (*The phone rings again.* HALLIDAY *slowly reaches for it and then violently rips it from its anchor*)

JERE (*After a brief pause*)   Oh, Mannie . . . What a brave thing to do!

94

HALLIDAY   Those attractive cannibals, they eat your time, they boil you alive in their pot of secondary pleasures and you find yourself enjoying the very stew you're cooking in.
   (*Voices are heard calling to them outside the cottage*)

GEORGETTE (*Off stage*)   Yoo-hoo.

FREDDY (*Off stage*)   Hallidays ahoy! (*Enter* FREDDY, *followed by* GEORGETTE, *both dressed nautically and carrying a bucket of champagne and glasses. They are attractively vivacious*) Had to see you. Had to see the convalescent.

JERE   Freddy, I'm awfully sorry. We're not seeing anyone yet.

GEORGETTE   But we have such wonderful news! To cheer both of you up.

HALLIDAY   Georgette! Can't you see we're not up to wonderful news.

FREDDY   What you need is some cheering up!

JERE   How did you ever find us?

GEORGETTE   Leave it to Freddy. I always say that if he loses his job at the studio he can become a detective—

FREDDY   It's because I know so many secrets that I keep my job, dear.

GEORGETTE We're on my honeymoon. I mean ours. We're being married tonight!

HALLIDAY Here? In La Jolla?

GEORGETTE On our boat! I'm going to become a mother!
(FREDDY *opens champagne bottle with a pop*)

JERE Darling, you have everything! A love-child and a husband.

GEORGETTE I can hardly believe that only two years ago I was an usher in the Bijou Theatre in Walla Walla.

HALLIDAY It could only happen in America.

FREDDY First it came as a shock. But I confess that I'm actually falling in love with her.

HALLIDAY You see your triumph, Georgette? You've finally aroused the monogamous in a congenital Don Juan.

FREDDY (*Pouring drinks*) Abysmal, frightfully out of character—but a toast to monogamy.

HALLIDAY To monogamy—but I'm afraid I better pass.

FREDDY *Mon ami,* how often do I enter matrimony and patrimony in the same ceremony? A touch, a ceremonial sip.

JERE It's only a sip of champagne.

GEORGETTE Champagne!

FREDDY It's your favorite Moet et Chandon twenty-one.

HALLIDAY (*Succumbing*) From the Piper Heidsieck shores of the Côte d'Azur ...

JERE To the Moet et Chandon beaches of La Jolla ...

HALLIDAY The popping of corks sets up a brave barrage.
  (*They drink gaily*)

JERE Such a lovely topaz taste! In these two weeks I'd almost forgotten.

GEORGETTE Freddy, let's have a child after every picture.

FREDDY (*Savoring the idea*) A promising agenda ... Now listen, children. I'm the director, you're the players. We open on the majestic, gleaming eighty-foot *Georgette Second* under full sail and bound for Caliente! The plot: a marriage at sea, and then a mad midnight wedding party at the Casino.

GEORGETTE   Co-starring our hosts, Dolores Costello and Jack Barrymore.

FREDDY   The morning after, which, by conservative calculation, will be around two in the afternoon, we'll have a champagne breakfast on board and there'll be sail-fishing for the sportsmen among us, and sleeping and love-making for the other ninety-nine percent.

JERE   It does sound heaven! Doesn't it, Mannie?

FREDDY   Now, you've got to hurry, you landlubbers. We should be casting off in fifteen minutes.

HALLIDAY (*Tempted*)   Freddy, you and Georgette First and Second are an enticing trinity—but there's my work . . .

FREDDY   Look, child, it's already Thursday! The weekend has begun!

GEORGETTE (*Hugging* HALLIDAY)   You've just got to come. If it's a boy, we're going to name him Manley.

HALLIDAY (*Weakening*)   I'd have to be back Monday morning first thing—and there isn't time to sail down there and back.

FREDDY   I'll have you flown from Caliente the minute you say so. Come on, Hallidays, the champagne is dwindling and the winds are freshening. We're on our way!

JERE   I've always loved big sailboats!. . . Remember our cruise with Bertie Bishop?

HALLIDAY   Those marvelous blue Greek islands!

JERE (*Pulling* HALLIDAY *up*)   Bertie kept making us do that awful dialogue from *The Sheik*. (*They fall into an embrace, burlesquing an old melodrama*) Take your compelling stare away from my bosom heaving under this soft silk.

HALLIDAY (*Now an exaggerated Barrymore*)   I know. I am a brute and a beast and a devil.

JERE   Are all Arabs hard like you? Has love never made you merciful?

HALLIDAY   Shall I make you love me? I can make women love me when I choose.
        (*They all laugh*)

FREDDY   Cut! We'll print that.

GEORGETTE   You simply have to do it on the boat tonight!

JERE   Oh, darling, should we go?

HALLIDAY (*After a pause*)   If you promise to be very good about reminding me on Monday morning.

GEORGETTE   You angels—that makes everything perfect!

FREDDY   All aboard for the good ship *Georgette Second!*

JERE (*Caught up in the old intoxication*)   What about clothes? I feel magenta!

GEORGETTE   I've a thousand rags on board—everything from bras to sables.

FREDDY   Just bring your lovely selves!

JERE   That's the way I adore to travel. (*They start to go*) One time in San Sebastián . . . Sylvester Ryan was passing our table and said, "Let's go, we're off to Bengal for a tiger hunt . . ." (*They exit, leaving* HALLIDAY *alone, and the present begins to return.* JERE *calls from off stage*) Mannie, you coming?
    (*Now* HALLIDAY *is in the attic room once more*)

HALLIDAY   Yes, I'm coming. I'm just having trouble finding my way.
    (*He staggers across the room, the groping convalescent of La Jolla becoming the drunken and ailing* HALLIDAY *of the present*)

STEARNS (*Entering rapidly*)   Manley, Milgrim just gave me hell but they're coming up here, so start thinking. We're about to get the heaveroo.

HALLIDAY Heaveroo? Never heard that word? You make it up? Or is it generic?

STEARNS (*Exacerbated and then frantic*) Who the hell cares what it is! I did my share. Now, come on, you do yours.

HALLIDAY Stick with me, laddie. Okay, Shep, okay, laddie. Help me.

STEARNS Help yourself. Save your own goddamn life. From here on in, I don't care what the hell happens to you.

HALLIDAY Stearns, tell you a secret ... Want Jere. Need Jere. Shep, do me a favor—call her. You got to call her.

STEARNS (*Sarcastically*) Anything you want!

HALLIDAY Want Jere. Want a new heart, a fresh start, a drink.
(*He shakily reaches into his valise for his tuxedo jacket and struggles into it while still sitting*)

STEARNS You've had a drink!

HALLIDAY Pour me a drink. Go on. I know what I'm doing. I'll drink myself on my feet. When this is all over with, I'll quit it. Like I quit it before. But right now I need a drink.
(STEARNS, *recognizing* HALLIDAY's *need, pours a drink. The chimes play a tune and strike five*)

STEARNS I hate that tune. I hate what time it is. I hate having to talk the story off the top of my head . . . Five o'clock in the afternoon.

HALLIDAY (*Pulling himself together*) The dinner for us, Saturday night, is black tie. Courage mounteth with occasion. (*Suddenly the broken wreck takes on the dignity of a deposed king*)

STEARNS The enemy approacheth.

HALLIDAY (*Grandly*) Kind and noble knight, you stir the conscience of your king. (*Earnestly*) I know the stakes, Shep— your young dream of conquest and my aging second-time-around grab at immortality. (*Voices are heard outside the door.* MILGRIM *enters and has time only for a brief look of disapproval as he is followed in by the Webster faculty group*)

MILGRIM (*Nervously*) This is where Mr. Halliday and young Stearns have been creating. I want you to meet the dean and his wife, Mrs. Llewellyn.

DEAN Mr. Halliday, how do you do!

MILGRIM Professor Connelly—he's the chairman of the English department, and Mrs. Connelly. And Mr. Ridgefield, in charge of public relations for the college.

HALLIDAY Welcome.

MILGRIM I trust you'll forgive the informality of Mr. Halliday's appearance. As I've told you, he's been working very hard.

DEAN (*Uneasily*) Of course, we quite understand.

CONNELLY Mr. Halliday, I don't know whether you remember it, but I met you some twenty years ago when we spoke at the New York convention of the Modern Language Association.

MRS. CONNELLY I was Richard's secretary. You kept trying to get me to come down to the bar with you.

HALLIDAY Richard Francis Connelly. I remember—you read a paper called the—the—"Further Comments on the Methodology of Syntax in the Later Novels of Henry James."

CONNELLY Remarkable memory!

HALLIDAY (*Dryly*) I also remember that those "Further Comments" took over an hour.

DEAN Mr. Halliday, we're very grateful to Mr. Milgrim for bringing you to us. Mrs. Llewellyn is especially grateful. She swears by you and Kenneth Roberts.

MRS. LLEWELLYN I read you for today and Mr. Roberts for yesterday.

HALLIDAY   Alas, who shall read me for tomorrow?

CONNELLY   I had occasion to reread several of your novels last summer and I must say you hold up surprisingly well.

HALLIDAY   Thank you. Won't you sit down please!
(*They sit down, grouped around* HALLIDAY)

RIDGEFIELD (*Holding pencil to pad*)   Mr. Halliday, if I can get a few quotes from you on the difference between writing novels and writing for the cinema I could 'hit the front pages of the Sunday *Times* and *Tribune* drama sections with a Webster dateline.

HALLIDAY   Yes—the difference between writing a novel and writing for the cinema—is . . .

RIDGEFIELD   Is. . .? Yes—is what?

HALLIDAY   Is, period . . . Close quotes.

DEAN   "Period. Close quotes." Very droll.

MRS. CONNELLY   You're pulling our leg.

CONNELLY   In the genre of Gertrude Stein.

104

MILGRIM (*Embarrassed*) Strange you should mention Gertrude Stein. I just cabled her to ask if she'd come over to do a picture for me.

HALLIDAY Four saints in three scenarios.

CONNELLY I suppose Shep told you that he chose your work for his final paper. He admired you very much—though he did see you as a classic decline of the middle-class artist.

HALLIDAY (*Looking sourly at* STEARNS) Well, I see him as the classic decline of the young leftist critic. Maybe the reason we admire each other so much is that we've been declining so much.
     (*He pats* STEARNS *affectionately*)

MILGRIM Well, I think we ought to begin. Now, you understand, Mr. Halliday will tell the story.

STEARNS (*Anxiously*) Mr. Milgrim, Manley and I decided that I'd take a stab at it, if it's all right with you—

MILGRIM Mr. Halliday will tell the story. In the rough, so to speak, but you'll have a general idea of where we're going.

CONNELLY Now, technically speaking, what stage is the movie in? Do you call what you have now a scenario or a photoplay?

HALLIDAY We call it the "Tentative Synthesis of an Anonymous Methodology."
     (*They laugh nervously*)

MILGRIM What we're working from now is a continuity breakdown—what we call a step sheet.

MRS. LLEWELLYN You know, I've never been behind the scenes of film-making before.

MILGRIM (*With forced assurance*) All ready? Curtain going up. We fade in. *Love on Ice*. Manley—Manley, you're on.
     (HALLIDAY *stares blankly at* MILGRIM)

STEARNS (*Jumping into the breach*) You see, we've got this ski captain—this ski captain—

MILGRIM (*Interrupting coldly*) Thank you, Stearns, but we've gathered here to listen to Manley Halliday. (STEARNS *moves back to stand beside* HALLIDAY) Manley, curtain's up and you're on.
     (HALLIDAY *fails to react*)

STEARNS (*Urgently, to* HALLIDAY) Blue sky-rack!

HALLIDAY (*He hears* STEARNS, *takes his hand, rises shakily, then after a long tense pause he begins to talk in an almost trance-like fashion*) We see a white fairyland in the Green Mountains. A tiny dark figure appears and starts sweeping down toward our camera. Faster and faster he flies over the freshly fallen snow, a perfect carpet for the Lone Skier. Youth charging down into the virgin field of trackless snow . . . (*He pauses. His audience is attentively silent*) At the bottom of this white world we see a winding road. Rounding into view comes an elegant touring car, carrying a single passenger, a girl whose face is aglow with the cold of the air and the warmth of being alive. She is the Princess Rimbaud. As her innocent, vivid young eyes lift to take in everything, she sees our skier, a breath-taking masculine blur of green against the snow-white slope . . .

MILGRIM (*Relieved and in an excited whisper*) Our cameraman can get that effect and make it both poetic and documentary.

MRS. LLEWELLYN It sounds breath-taking!

MRS. CONNELLY He's a natural storyteller!

STEARNS Manley, you've got hold of the rack!

HALLIDAY (*Unhearing, in his own world*) At the same time a sudden graceful *Gelandersprung* offers our hero his first sight of the girl. In a flash he sees the pride, the ardor, the lovely glow, the golden curls. We cut to her haunting unforgettable face. "I feel so opalescent white," she says. Arrested by this vision our skier checks his flight, and his skis throw up behind him a dazzling white fan of flying crystals. The car has come abreast of the Lone Skier now. Slowly the girl taps the glass between the chauffeur and herself. The car comes to a stop. She looks unashamedly at the skier. For a moment as pure and still as the trackless snow they look questioningly into each other's eyes. At one glance they meet, love, marry, age together and die. Lowering her eyes at last, the girl reaches forward with poised reluctance and signals the chauffeur. And as the touring car drives off, the golden girl, who is really the Goddess of So-Near-and-Yet-So-Far, a lovely Miss-As-Good-As-a-Mile, flings her head for a last defiant, yet regretful view of her lost skier. Then she moves off into the bright morning, into the future, and he skis on toward other virgin fields beyond, into her past. Boy and girl forever losing, finding and not keeping, even in Fairyland.

MRS. LLEWELLYN (*Whispering*) Marvelous!

MRS. CONNELLY (*To her husband*) It's a wistful pastel!

STEARNS Go on, Manley, keep going.
(HALLIDAY *falters a little*)

MILGRIM The boy, the girl, they meet . . . and—

HALLIDAY (*After a trembling pause*) And . . . and they never see each other again.

MILGRIM (*Standing up in bewilderment*) Never see each other again! But that's just an introduction, an opening sequence. It's good but there's got to be more!
(HALLIDAY *turns somnambulistically and makes for the door*)

STEARNS (*Blocking his path at the door*)   Manley, where are you going?

HALLIDAY   I'm going to Jere.

STEARNS   Where?

HALLIDAY   I'm going to see Jere!

STEARNS (*Pleadingly*)   Come on, Manley, finish it!

MILGRIM (*Angrily*)   Finish it! I insist that you finish it.

STEARNS   Just hang on to the rack.

MILGRIM   Manley, there's got to be more!

HALLIDAY (*Slowly coming back to reality*)   You want more?

MRS. CONNELLY   Yes of course we do!

MRS. LLEWELLYN   Yes! Yes!

HALLIDAY (*Uncertainly*)   I'll give you more. From the slick surface of the ski jump—(*With growing certainty and mounting demoniacal frenzy*)—we dissolve to the slick surface of the faculty mind. From the beautiful snow-white surface of a ski trail we dissolve to the hand of Victor Milgrim as it moves up the beautiful snowy-white surface of a thigh—of Mrs. Connelly's thigh. And as Victor Milgrim's hand moves up and up and up . . .

(STEARNS *seizes hold of* HALLIDAY's *too-graphic hand. There is general chaos in the room*)

MILGRIM I don't know when the next train leaves, but you two bastards better be on it!

HALLIDAY (*Shouting*) I told you there wasn't any more. It was all over, finished, a lifetime in a minute. Pure poetry and pure crap. Exactly right for a movie script. Now this party is over . . . done . . . *fini* . . . *kaput!* Out!

DEAN (*As the rest of his group hurry out, shocked*) I seriously doubt that Webster can have anything further to do with this project.

(*He exits.* HALLIDAY, STEARNS *and* MILGRIM *are alone in the room*)

MILGRIM (*Confronting* HALLIDAY) Now put it in your memoir, how the great author was victimized by a Hollywood ignoramus.

HALLIDAY No, Victor . . . I said I would give up ten weeks of my life to gain ten months for my work and that's the way the Devil works. Because your life is not your own to bargain away and all the Devils know it. Poor innocent Faust. I was not even sad, only miserable. Not noble, only ignoble. Not wise, only clever. Not substantial, only a silhouette. Not tensile, only brittle. Not dedicated, only obsessed. Poor stupid Faust. The moment you make that bargain you're undone. In that first minute, in that instant. The mistake was then —not now. In the beginning . . . not in the end. You see, that's the Holy Ghost . . . he isn't in man as a presence, but bargain with your life and you feel him as an absence . . . and what a vacancy it is.

MILGRIM Manley, it's too late for anger. I leave you to—yourself.
    (*He exits.* STEARNS *starts to leave*)

HALLIDAY (*Wildly, close to delirium*) Shep, I loused it up for you. Let you down. Let Milgrim down. He had to be so goddamn intellectual, bringing me up here to dangle on his vest like a Phi Beta key . . . a living classic!

STEARNS (*Turns to* HALLIDAY *at the door*) Once, when I heard you were alive, and going to work on *Love on Ice,* I couldn't believe it. I thought you were dead. (*His voice rising, he approaches* HALLIDAY)—You are dead, aren't you? Tell me . . . are you dead?

HALLIDAY (*Barely able to stand, inviting a blow*) Go ahead . . . hit me. It'll make you feel more noble. You bastard! Go ahead! Hit me! (STEARNS *moves in furiously to strike* HALLIDAY. *Just as he is about to hit out, he suddenly thrusts forward with a burst of love and understanding and embraces* HALLIDAY. HALLIDAY *begins to sink down and* STEARNS *helps him to the couch. He is gasping for breath and groans in pain*) Oh,

Lord. Shall we never be done growing? Will I never say, quietly, It's the beginning. Now I begin. Today an old man makes a young start?

STEARNS Hang on, Manley. I'll get a doctor.
(*He rushes out*)

HALLIDAY (*In a final effort, he begins to write, and then stops as though hallucinated*) Jere!. . . Jere!. . . This time . . . this time! (*The phantom* JERE *of the twenties appears behind him, accompanied by the faint tinkle of long-remembered music*) Jere, that dress—it's on fire! It flashes and shimmers!

JERE One of these days you'll want me back. Will you love me soon? And make me feel Venetian red? Say no, and I won't go. Waltz me at midnight to the *Rosenkavalier*. I love to dive deep, I need to climb high. Ish kabibble. I see the world spinning. I see inside you spinning.

HALLIDAY (*Shouting hoarsely*) Take her away! Take her away! This woman is smothering me!

JERE I feel champagne—
(HALLIDAY *falls back dead, the pencil drops from his hand and simultaneously the vision disappears*)

STEARNS (*Re-enters*) Manley, the doctor's coming—he—
(STEARNS *realizes that* HALLIDAY *is dead. Overcome, he backs away across the room toward the window. Seeing the typewriter, he grabs it up violently and raises it over his head in*

order to smash it to the ground, as though with this act he can obliterate the tormented life of MANLEY HALLIDAY—*perhaps even literature itself. As he stands ready to hurl the typewriter, he notices a slip of paper clutched in* HALLIDAY's *hand. He puts the typewriter down on the table, goes to* HALLIDAY *and gently takes the paper from the lifeless hand, and reads slowly*) "A second chance—that was our delusion. A first chance—that's all we have. Remember that, laddie—" (*He crumples the paper harshly and then, with deep anguish and increasing resolution, he reassures his dead friend*) Okay, laddie, okay, okay, okay—

Curtain

A40